Change the way you move!

A central business district goes ecomobile

Tobias Kuttler | Theresa Zimmermann

Konrad Otto-Zimmermann (ed.)

"You are not *in* traffic, you *are* traffic."

Executive Mayor Mpho Parks Tau

Contents

Preface

Parks Tau, the executive mayor of Johannesburg, South Africa, took a bold decision. His city needed to overcome the socio-spatial divide of earlier apartheid planning. Ever-increasing congestion in and around the Sandton Central Business District (CBD) needed to be addressed. Johannesburg is committed to contributing—in concert with other world cities—to global climate change mitigation by reducing CO_2 emissions, and is determined to tackle automobile traffic as a major source of pollution.

The decision to host the EcoMobility World Festival 2015 and to organise it in partnership with ICLEI in the Sandton Central Business District—often referred to as Africa's richest square mile—expressed the courageous determination to broach the way citizens move and to come to grips with 75,000 commuters who drive their cars into Sandton every day, calling upon them to "change the way you move".

An EcoMobility Festival is a month-long *mise-en-scène* of urban mobility and transport, as we would like to see it in the future. It is the temporary transformation of infrastructure and traffic regulations to make citizens switch from the private automobile to using public transport, cycling, and walking. It invites citizens to try out behavioural change and to collectively experience a different scenario of urban mobility.

Neither the festival nor this book would have come into existence without the visionary dedication and support from Executive Mayor Parks Tau, Member of the Mayoral Committee Christine Walters, and Executive Director for Transport Lisa Seftel, as well as dozens of City of Johannesburg staff members. The book draws on survey data, evaluation reports, and charts provided by City departments and their service providers. Notably, the authors have accompanied individual citizens on their commutes to Sandton CBD on foot, by minibus taxi, bus, and train, and interviewed them about their commuting experiences. The book also reflects insights and opinions the authors gained through interviews and conversations with business leaders, young entrepreneurs, university teachers, NGO activists, and people in the streets. Without being able to mention the names of all direct and indirect contributors, I wish to acknowledge their invaluable input with gratitude.

Lastly, I wish to commend the authors, Tobias Kuttler and Theresa Zimmermann—who witnessed and reported on the first EcoMobility Festival in Suwon 2013—for this comprehensive portrait of the unique EcoMobility World Festival 2015 in Johannesburg.

Konrad Otto-Zimmermann
Creative director, EcoMobility World Festivals

The experiences in Johannesburg are shared through this book publication, a Festival Report, and a website. Furthermore, film documentaries are available for online viewing or download.

A CBD Goes Ecomobile,
15min. URL https://vimeo.com/155287316

Moving Together: Social Integration through Ecomobility,
10min. URL https://vimeo.com/155280459

EcoMobility Festivals Gateway
www.ecomobilityfestival.net

Aim and structure of this book

The second edition of the EcoMobility World Festival came to the right place, at the right moment in time. The decision to host the festival in 2015, just prior to the twenty-first United Nations Climate Change Conference COP21 in Paris, directed the attention of experts and the public to Johannesburg. The strong statement made in support of urban ecomobility has demonstrated how global cities like Johannesburg, London, New York, Seoul, and Tokyo are determined to tackle climate change, air pollution, and traffic gridlock through innovative solutions.

Keeping in mind global challenges, this book wants to inspire decision-makers, planners, and the public by portraying the activities of the EcoMobility World Festival 2015 and the city's vision for the future of Johannesburg. There are many reasons to have a closer look at recent developments in this city-region: the city administration has decided to play a role in the global combat against climate change, and at the same time tackle the city's problems in a very determined and holistic way. To combine these purposes, the local government has created a vision for an equitable and inclusive city that builds on ecomobility as critical interface between different aspects of sustainable urban development.

This book portrays the city and its actors. It documents the festival project and the process of engaging with citizens, involving stakeholders, and partnering with like-minded institutions. Furthermore, it presents the festival in the context of Johannesburg's transport-related spheres of activity:

- Decongestion of dense city quarters (especially Sandton CBD), including change of travel behaviour and reducing car dependency
- Socio-spatial reorganisation ("restitching") of the city-region: ecomobility tackles inequality and in the long term reduces spatial segregation; it brings citizens together in public transport and street spaces and allows social interaction
- Creating vibrant public spaces: prioritising ecomobility means reclaiming space from cars and working towards a harmonious relationship between mobility and other uses in open space
- Collaborating with governments, business, and citizens: sustainable urban development relies on a shared vision of urban society for the future of the city, on partnerships and mutual agreements
- Global climate change mitigation and adaptation: global cities are substantial sources of CO_2 emissions, but also important innovators in urban climate policies

The book begins with a portrait of the festival, its objectives, components, and messages. The following chapters deal with the different spheres of urban development by highlighting the role of ecomobility in building sustainable cities. Each thematic chapter gives a short overview of global challenges and approaches, and presents in detail how the City tackled its specific challenges

and used the approaches that the festival offered as part of the solution. The results chapter discusses successful measures as well as shortcomings, and reports how the modes of commuting changed during the festival. The book concludes with a description of the legacy projects that the City envisages based on the experiences and lessons learnt from the festival.

The authors spent several weeks in Johannesburg before, during, and after the festival to experience the festival atmosphere; to speak to experts, participants, and organisers; and to accompany commuters on their daily journeys. The international experts who are quoted in this book participated in the EcoMobility Dialogues.

1 Johannesburg
EcoMobility Festival at a glance

Festival Key Facts

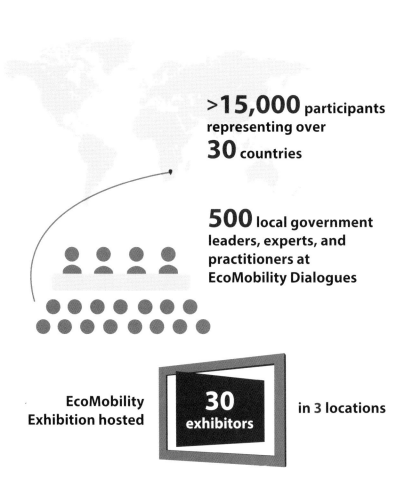

>**15,000** participants representing over **30** countries

500 local government leaders, experts, and practitioners at EcoMobility Dialogues

EcoMobility Exhibition hosted **30 exhibitors** in 3 locations

>**350** vehicles and **10,000** visitors at Expo Online

2,300 children learn and experience new things at the exhibition

 16 million social media impressions for #joburgecomobility

 nearly **10%** more Gautrain users compared to October 2014

 15 minutes **of commuter time-saving through Park & Ride and managed lanes**

 22% less private car use

 **5x** more pedestrians in festival area

What is ecomobility?

Car-dominated cities have no future. Cars are basically metal cans that have ten to forty times the weight of the passenger they carry. On average, cars are only used during 5 per cent of the time, while during the other 95 per cent they block valuable urban space. When the amount of work is considered that is necessary to earn the money that is spent on the purchase, repair, parking, etc. of cars, the calculation of the ratio of distance travelled to time spent is rather unpleasant: the average speed of the car is not more than four to eight kilometres per hour. Furthermore, cars with combustion engines contribute to the acceleration of climate change. This cannot be called an efficient means of transport; thus a radical change is unavoidable.

"Ecomobility" is the term for the green alternative to the automobile-dominated transport systems and mobility patterns in our cities. According to Konrad Otto-Zimmermann of The Urban Idea, "Ecomobility, a term we coined in 2007, denotes the entirety of walking, cycling and wheeling, and 'passenging'—i.e.,

using public transport. Car sharing may fall under ecomobility, provided cars are small, light city vehicles powered by renewable energy." The word "ecomobility" implies mobility that is ecologically sound and economically favourable, and thus eco-efficient. As ICLEI phrases it, it is "travel through integrated, socially inclusive, and environmentally friendly options".

Ecomobility applies the subsidiarity principle to both the individual choice of transport mode for each trip, and to urban transport policy and planning: as an individual, walk; where you can't walk, go by bicycle; where the bicycle can't help, use public transport. If you still need a car for a specific purpose, use a vehicle from a car-sharing service. As a policymaker or planner, plan for a walkable city. Also create a network of safe cycleways, as well as bike sharing, parking, and bike-and-ride infrastructure. In addition, provide an attractive public transport system.

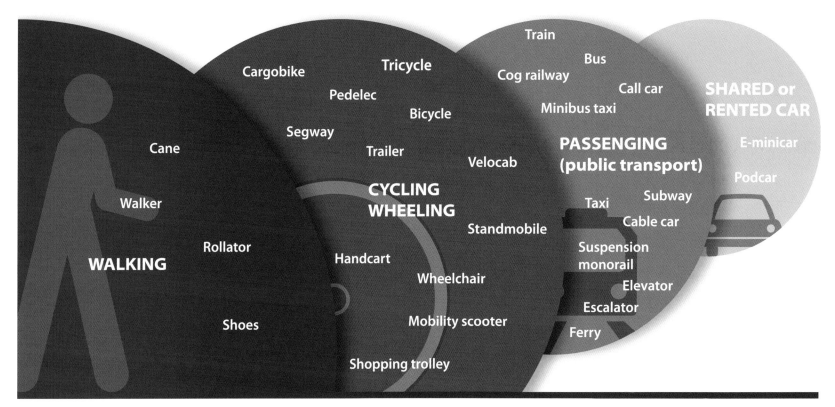

Subsidiarity in urban transport:
the priority order for individual modal choice, transport policy, and infrastructure planning

An ecomobile CBD: turning a challenge into an opportunity

Pedestrians, bicycles, and Segways on the streets where cars usually crawl along. Food stalls, concerts, and sports events along the roads where cars used to park. People of different backgrounds enjoying the space together that once entirely belonged to motor vehicles. This vision has become reality in one of the world's most dynamic business centres, the Sandton Central Business District (CBD), one of Johannesburg's two large commercial hubs.

Inner-city business districts all over the world suffer from congestion, air pollution, and noise. Once economies grow, business activities increase, and the business districts become more densely built up, these problems often become unbearable. Globally connected business hubs—the flagships and backbones of today's national economies—are then on the verge of becoming uncompetitive due the local constraints.

In some cases, the high density of activities, people, and buildings in CBDs is a problem when it is not well steered and organised; however, this density is an opportunity when administered well. As a spatial form, the CBD is highly suited to an efficient, comfortable, reliable, and safe integrated transport system. Mass transit plays a major role in accommodating the needs of the majority of commuters. Moreover, there is a trend among young urban professionals in leading healthy and eco-friendly lifestyles, with the effect that walking and cycling as commuting choices are becoming increasingly popular.

CBDs are suitable places to spread innovations and new messages. They attract thousands of people from all over the metropolitan region. New developments at the workplace are discussed at home, in the neighbourhood, and at the sports club. Furthermore, CBDs are not only at the centre of local attention, but are also observed closely by global economic and political elites.

The EcoMobility World Festival 2015 in Sandton, Johannesburg has presented a *mise-en-scène* of an ecomobile central business district. Johannesburg has proven that a densely built-up inner-city district can prioritise ecomobility. More than that, it has been proven that an ecomobile CBD is more attractive as a place to live and work, and the quality of public spaces improves in numerous ways. The festival has seen car commuters changing to ecomobile options and has convinced them that travelling in an ecomobile fashion can be even more convenient, safe, and reliable than private cars. Thus, the festival has achieved its first objective: convincing people to change the way they move. It further succeeded in making people talk about transport, urban life, and sustainability. The festival gained attention in the whole of South Africa and other parts of the world. The local, national, and global media attention was unprecedented, with every aspect and development during the planning process and the festival period being fiercely and often controversially discussed in print, web, radio, and television media. The overwhelming attention and popularity of the festival on social media shows that the debates moved many more citizens than just Sandton employees and residents.

△
Daily rush-hour traffic in Johannesburg CBD

"Obviously the people that we wanted the most to change the way they move are car users. But what we also wanted is that the word ecomobility is on everybody's lips. I think we have been able to touch everybody."

Lisa Seftel, executive director for transport,
City of Johannesburg

Mpho Franklyn Parks Tau
Executive mayor of the City of Johannesburg

City of Johannesburg Executive Mayor Cllr. Parks Tau is the mastermind behind the 2015 edition of the EcoMobility World Festival. Mayor Tau's vision for his city and his love for its communities and their sustainability for generations to come saw him take up the global initiative. His belief in the contribution that Johannesburg can make to the circle of grand world cities continuously sees him working for the advancement of the people and the positioning of the African city in the global community.

Mpho Franklyn Parks Tau is the second democratically elected executive mayor of the City of Johannesburg. Growing up in Soweto under the system of racial segregation enforced by the apartheid regime from 1947 to 1994, Tau became a political activist at an early age. He took up leadership roles in anti-apartheid organisations, such as the Congress of South African Students (Cosas) and the Soweto Youth Congress. At the tipping point of the liberation struggle, he was by the side of the great leaders of the struggle who inspired his personal development. Since 2000, Mayor Tau has been a member of the Mayoral Committee of Johannesburg. In 2011, he assumed office as executive mayor and began driving Johannesburg's spatial and socio-economic transformation.

Strategic Leader

Parks Tau's vision for Johannesburg is that of an equitable and liveable city, which he defines as "a place that creates opportunities for everybody who wants to access the city and its cultural, social, and economic amenities". A liveable city is also "a city that you can interact with— [where people have] the ability to get into the street, be a part of the city, and interact with [other] people". In order to improve citizens' access to economic opportunities, Parks Tau translated his vision into the ambitious "Corridors of Freedom" – a programme designed to reverse the spatial injustices of apartheid.

Mayor Tau is a vocal proponent of building a more environmentally sustainable infrastructure for the city, while creating awareness about conservation and a modern city's need to adapt to a new climate reality. His commitment to the environment has resulted in Mayor Tau taking up international leadership. Johannesburg's long-standing involvement with ICLEI – Local Governments for Sustainability, the international association of local and metropolitan governments dedicated to sustainable development, led to the hosting of the EcoMobility World Festival.

Mayor Tau's enthusiasm for the festival project was ignited as early as 2012, when the creative director and initiator of the festival idea, Konrad Otto-Zimmermann, described the concept to him. Mayor Tau was convinced that hosting the EcoMobility World Festival 2015 supported his vision for an eco-friendly, inclusive, and innovative city. And being a regular cyclist, Mayor Tau is convinced that change starts with one's own behavioural adjustment. Consequently, during the festival, Mayor Tau commuted from his home in the south of Johannesburg by public transport to Sandton in northern Johannesburg, where he had temporarily moved his office.

Johannesburg: a mining town becomes a global city

Johannesburg is a young city; it was established in 1886, two years after the Witwatersrand gold reef was discovered. The rush of fortune-seekers caused the city population to grow to 100,000 within ten years, making it one of the fastest-growing cities ever.

The city's history is closely linked to the history of apartheid. Already in the early days of Johannesburg, the municipal authorities sought to keep the different racial groups separated. In 1913, the British colonial government began to implement formal racial segregation by passing the Land Act, which marked the beginning of a system that later became known as apartheid. Africans living in the central city were forcibly relocated to townships far from places of work and where whites lived.

In the south-west of Johannesburg, a large township was established. African people were forcibly moved to this area and lost their freehold titles. Soweto, short for South Western Townships, became one of the centres of rebellion against apartheid. One of the residents of Orlando (a Soweto township) was Nelson Mandela, who went on to play a central role in the liberation of South Africa.

Since South Africa became a democratic country in 1994, the city has undergone significant changes. In order to tackle the region's fragmentation, the city's boundaries were extended to include former townships as well as wealthy suburbs. In 2000, Johannesburg was restructured to become a single metropolitan authority. New governance models and policies were implemented that support poverty alleviation, provide equal service delivery and basic services to all, and spur economic growth.

The creation of a stable and credibly operating city government was the foundation for Johannesburg's recent economic success and its rise to a global city. From an important mining centre, Johannesburg has developed into the primary economic and financial hub of southern Africa. It is home to the largest stock exchange on the continent. More than two-thirds of South African companies have their headquarters in Johannesburg, and the city creates 16.5 per cent of the country's wealth. The city became a hotspot for sustainable urban development and its innovative contributions are increasingly recognised all over the world.

Key Facts Johannesburg
Population (2011): 4.43 million (racial breakdown by percentage: 76.4 African, 12.3 white, 5.6 coloured, 4.9 Indian)
Annual growth rate: 3.2 per cent
Unemployment rate: 28 per cent
Average household incomes (2011):
- African: R 68,000 (approx. EUR 4,000)
- Coloured: R 142,000 (approx. EUR 8,300)
- Indian/Asian: R 259,000 (approx. EUR 15,100)
- White: R 360,000 (approx. EUR 21,000)

◁ The cooling towers of the former Orlando Power Station are an important landmark in Soweto.

◁ In October, the jacaranda trees blossom and turn the suburbs of Johannesburg purple.

Sandton: "Africa's richest square mile"

The Sandton CBD is the epicentre of Johannesburg's economic success story. Directly between Johannesburg CBD and Tshwane, Sandton is located in the heart of a dynamic economic corridor. In close proximity to the city's international airport, Sandton has gradually replaced Johannesburg's older CBD in the inner city as the most important finance and commercial centre. Often referred to as "Africa's richest square mile", Sandton is the prime office location in Gauteng Province and hosts many of the corporate headquarters for South Africa or southern Africa.

Until the nineteen-seventies, Sandton was largely a farming and smallholding community. Land prices were significantly cheaper than in other parts of Johannesburg. In 1973, the Sandton City Shopping Centre and office towers opened their doors. This development kicked off the transformation into a business hub, which has continuously grown in size and importance since then.

Apart from its role as popular shopping destination, Sandton is also noted for its international convention centre, which is one of the largest on the continent. It was the site of the 2002 World Summit on Sustainable Development ("Rio+10"), and Nelson Mandela Square—with a giant statute of the political leader—is a popular tourist destination and a distinguished location for culinary art and nightlife.

"Sandton is beautiful, it has a very cool atmosphere. There are many security guards going around, so there are no robberies here, not even at night-time. I like to be here in Sandton."
Polly, 63 years old, works in a hotel in Sandton

▽
Nelson Mandela Square in Sandton

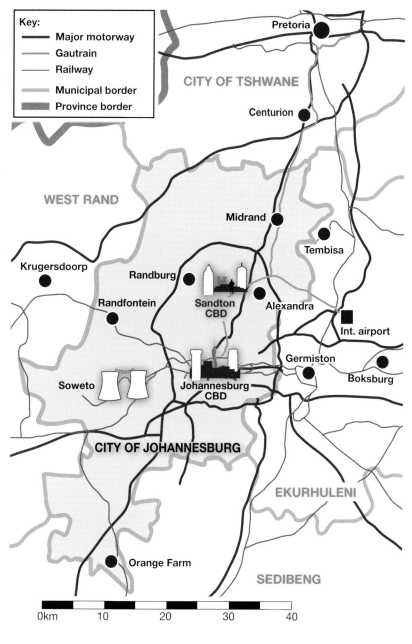

Christine Walters, member of Mayoral Committee for transport, City of Johannesburg

Councillor Christine Walters is a member of the Mayoral Committee (MMC), the local government cabinet of the City of Johannesburg. Since February 2013, Christine Walters has overseen the transport department, including the Johannesburg Roads Agency as well as the municipal transport provider Metrobus. In this role, she intensively supported the EcoMobility World Festival and personally held many dialogues with citizens and stakeholders prior to the event.

Christine Walters has always understood herself foremost as a community worker: "This year I am celebrating having dedicated my life to the struggle for fifty-two years. I have a great love for people." She has been part of the Alexandra community since 1994, where she has worked to better the lives of people from this community ever since. "Even if I am a member of the Mayoral Committee, I still love the work in my community. I assist in resolving political issues in our area and empowering young people. My whole dedication is for the liberation and emancipation of our people."

She has been involved in the struggle for democracy and in community work since the age of fourteen, after her family was forcibly removed from the suburbs of Cape Town. While she worked in the clothing industry from 1967 to 1975, she became involved in organising workers and was active in the Young Christians Workers Movement, where she educated office, factory, and domestic workers on their rights and how to challenge the status quo.

During her studies at the University of Oxford in the nineteen-seventies, she was an executive member of the Student Representative Council at the Plato College and later became director of the only Community Arts Centre for Black Artists in Cape Town.

In 1987, Walters relocated to Johannesburg, which she describes as the place where she "found her spirit and love". While working in the banking sector, she continued social and political activism and was an active member of South Africa's largest umbrella organisation for trade unions (COSATU). Following the 1994 transition, she became a councillor for Sandton, and since then has been councillor continuously for over twenty years. In 2000, Walters was appointed as member of the Mayoral Committee (MMC) and played an important role in the committee responsible for the city's human development strategy.

One of Walters' biggest concerns is that many South Africans still live in poverty. She is convinced that quality transport infrastructure can make a huge difference. "Every month, we have over 420,000 people going hungry in the city. If you look at the poorest people's budget, the bulk of their money goes to transport. The city is still spatially divided based on the apartheid design, so transport plays a major role in creating the backbone. That is why we are creating Corridors of Freedom by implementing the BRT and building infrastructure for non-motorised transport all over Johannesburg."

▽
Christine Walters (right), Gauteng Premier David Makhura (centre), and Ismail Vadi, MEC for roads and transport of Gauteng Province (left) explore the festival area.

Champion for Cohesion in the City

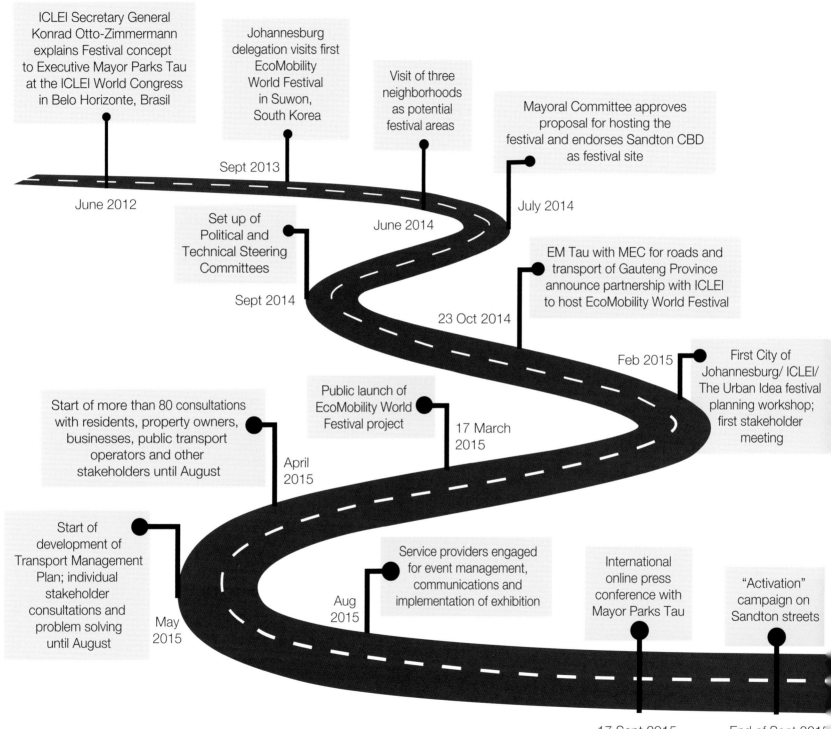

ICLEI Secretary General Konrad Otto-Zimmermann explains Festival concept to Executive Mayor Parks Tau at the ICLEI World Congress in Belo Horizonte, Brasil

June 2012

Johannesburg delegation visits first EcoMobility World Festival in Suwon, South Korea

Sept 2013

Visit of three neighborhoods as potential festival areas

June 2014

Mayoral Committee approves proposal for hosting the festival and endorses Sandton CBD as festival site

July 2014

Set up of Political and Technical Steering Committees

Sept 2014

EM Tau with MEC for roads and transport of Gauteng Province announce partnership with ICLEI to host EcoMobility World Festival

23 Oct 2014

First City of Johannesburg/ ICLEI/ The Urban Idea festival planning workshop; first stakeholder meeting

Feb 2015

Start of more than 80 consultations with residents, property owners, businesses, public transport operators and other stakeholders until August

April 2015

Public launch of EcoMobility World Festival project

17 March 2015

Start of development of Transport Management Plan; individual stakeholder consultations and problem solving until August

May 2015

Service providers engaged for event management, communications and implementation of exhibition

Aug 2015

International online press conference with Mayor Parks Tau

17 Sept 2015

"Activation" campaign on Sandton streets

End of Sept 2015

14

The way towards the festival

The EcoMobility World Festival 2015 in Johannesburg was a giant leap forward in the City's endeavour to foster sustainable urban development and an integrated public transport system. It is also the outcome of a long-standing relationship with ICLEI – Local Governments for Sustainability, the organisation that partnered with the City to organise the festival.

Additionally, it is the result of two visionaries meeting and exchanging ideas: when Konrad Otto-Zimmermann, creative director of The Urban Idea, initiator of the festival idea and former ICLEI general secretary, explained the festival concept to the mayor in 2012, Parks Tau was immediately interested. The Johannesburg cabinet members responsible for transport, Rehana Moosajee and—from the beginning of 2013—Christine Walters, took the project forward. In September 2013, Johannesburg sent a three-member delegation of city staff members to Suwon, South Korea, to witness and report back from the first EcoMobility World Festival. Encouraged by the success of the Suwon Festival, the discussion gained momentum. In mid-2014, the Mayoral Committee approved the proposal of hosting the Festival 2015 during the month of October, which has been Transport Month in South Africa since 2005 and promotes safe, affordable, accessible, and reliable transport in the country. Several locations for the festival were under scrutiny: Maboneng Precinct,

Melville, and Sandton CBD. Mayor Tau preferred Sandton and convinced his team and the partners of this site. They knew that while having the festival in Sandton could have a huge impact, it would also be a challenge. Above all, many representatives of Sandton's business community had doubts about the festival, but over many months of conversations with local stakeholders, support for the project grew steadily. The business community of Sandton had also long realised that something needs to be done about the traffic.

The fact that the business community joined his endeavour didn't surprise Mayor Tau: "Johannesburg is not a timid city. Sandton is not a place for hesitant or tentative people. We are bold and brash. We are imaginative and filled with self-confidence. This part of town has become the richest square mile in Africa because of people who took risks and staked their claims on the future."

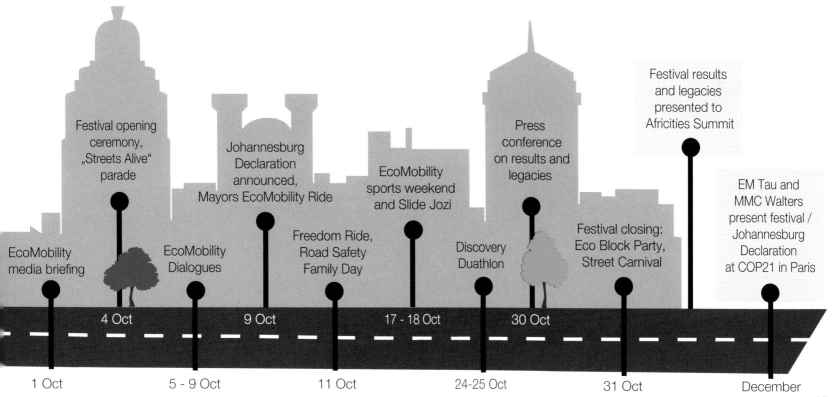

EcoMobility media briefing — 1 Oct

Festival opening ceremony, „Streets Alive" parade — 4 Oct

EcoMobility Dialogues — 5 - 9 Oct

Johannesburg Declaration announced, Mayors EcoMobility Ride — 9 Oct

Freedom Ride, Road Safety Family Day — 11 Oct

EcoMobility sports weekend and Slide Jozi — 17 - 18 Oct

Discovery Duathlon — 24-25 Oct

Press conference on results and legacies — 30 Oct

Festival closing: Eco Block Party, Street Carnival — 31 Oct

Festival results and legacies presented to Africities Summit

EM Tau and MMC Walters present festival / Johannesburg Declaration at COP21 in Paris — December

"It takes courage and leadership to make change, especially in the face of adversity. The city has an obligation to its commuters, but also to the environment. We are trying to find the balance between easing congestion on our roads and creating a more sustainable lifestyle. Of course with change, there will come a little bit of pain; that is inevitable. We are not only taking people out of their comfort zone, we are changing the paradigm. The festival will act as a catalyst, other cities will follow."

Kadri Nassiep, CEO, South African National
Energy Development Institute (SANEDI)

Festival objectives

- Enable behavioural change from private car use towards ecomobility
- Kick-start the process of decongesting Sandton
- Showcase infrastructural interventions to promote ecomobility
- Promote Johannesburg as a cycle-friendly city
- Show and promote other non-motorised and alternatively powered vehicles as means of mobility
- Increase the patronage of Rea Vaya Bus Rapid Transit, Metrobus, and other forms of quality public transport
- Show the benefits of reduced congestion and ecomobility for productivity, quality of life, air quality, and emission standards
- Promote walking and cycling (and other ecomobile modes) as part of a healthy and sustainable lifestyle

"By having the festival in Sandton, we made sure that we touch more residents than in any other part of the city. Also, we are positively affecting the many people travelling in public transport for many hours from different parts of the city into Sandton."

Lisa Seftel, executive director for transport,
City of Johannesburg

▽
From left to right: Christine Walters (MMC for transport, City of Johannesburg), Monika Zimmermann (ICLEI), Tae-young Yeom (mayor of Suwon, South Korea), David Makhura (premier, Gauteng Province), Dipuo Peters (minister of transport, SA), Ismail Vadi (MEC for roads and transport, Gauteng), Parks Tau (executive mayor, City of Johannesburg) cut the ribbon to officially start the EcoMobility World Festival 2015.

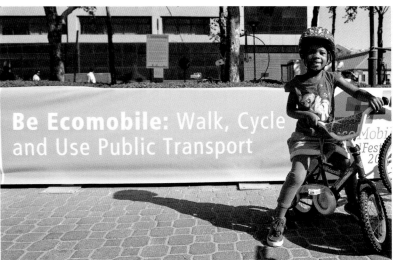

Main festival aspects

Transport Management Plan and legacy projects

In order to reduce congestion in and around Sandton, the City of Johannesburg developed an ambitious Transport Management Plan for the festival month. This plan aimed at providing ecomobile alternatives to travelling by car. By putting in place such a system for one month, the citizens of Johannesburg could experience what a future comprehensive transport system based on the principles of ecomobility could look and feel like.

The transport management for the festival included measures for commuting to and from Sandton as well as for moving in an ecomobile way inside the Sandton CBD. This was made possible by the closure of certain streets in the CBD, the introduction of managed priority lanes for public transport, restructuring of traffic flows, installation of bicycle lanes, enhanced train and bus services, and communication and education activities.

As a legacy of the festival, the City of Johannesburg has been implementing ten projects to translate the temporary transport experiments into lasting measures that will shape the city's mobility future. The legacy projects are also embedded in Johannesburg's continuing efforts to reshape the city, as envisioned in the "Corridors of Freedom" master plan.

EcoMobility Exhibition

A month-long exhibition was held in Sandton and Alexandra during the festival period. It was organised to show new modes of movement and to educate consumers on vehicle options for greener mobility in our cities and towns. The exhibition included thirty exhibitors and innovative entrepreneurs as well as a test track, on which citizens could test ride about seventy vehicles.

Groups from schools, orphanages, universities, businesses, and the government visited the exhibition and enjoyed educational events, such as storytelling and science education workshops. Trained volunteers guided the visitors through the interactive museum "Our History of Transport" and a mobile exhibition.

Seminars and presentations on bike sharing, urban cable cars, and e-bikes were hosted along with the exhibition. In parallel, the EcoMobility Expo Online displayed over 350 types of ecomobility vehicles and received over 10,000 online visitors during the festival month.

During the Mayors' EcoMobility Ride, about fifty international and local city leaders and other participants paraded with a variety of ecomobile vehicles. It was a visible statement about what a future, human-scale urban transport could look like.

EcoMobility Dialogues

The EcoMobility Dialogues—organised by ICLEI in partnership with the City from 5–9 October 2015—brought together hundreds of participants, including nearly fifty speakers from twenty countries in Africa, Asia, Latin America, Europe, and North America. Decision-makers and practitioners, local and international experts, academics and media experts exchanged and promoted innovative thinking on urban planning and transport issues.

The EcoMobility Dialogues included workshops on the latest advances in sustainable transport approaches—including transport demand management, clean bus fleets, integrated urban and transport planning, and shared forms of mobility. The *Imbizo*—a public dialogue with the executive mayor—gave citizens of Johannesburg the opportunity to interact directly with the mayor and a panel of experts. The debates included topics such as linking urban planning with the development of sustainable transport, road safety, social inclusion, and the challenges of a car-centric culture.

The Johannesburg Declaration on EcoMobility in Cities was formulated and adopted at the Leaders Roundtable, which was attended by mayors, deputy mayors, heads of transport, and topic experts from around the world. It was presented in Paris during the twenty-first United Nations Climate Change Conference, COP21.

Events

The festival presented activities to showcase a people-friendly business district with active street life and a socially inclusive mobility system. Each weekend, a major event took place in and around Sandton, with the central axis, West Street, and other adjacent streets being closed. Around 15,000 people from various communities across Johannesburg attended the events and experienced the economic hub in a very different way.

Linking communities that are spatially divided was the objective of the Streets Alive cycling and walking parade between the Sandton CBD and Alexandra, a residential area and one of the poorest parts of the city.

During the Freedom Ride, 4,000 cyclists enjoyed their Sunday morning by claiming almost thirty kilometres of streets linking Sandton with the inner-city district of Hillbrow and the township of Alexandra. At the Road Safety Family Day, families experienced picnicking, dancing, and playing in the streets while learning about road safety.

During the Sporting Weekend, West Street hosted sport competitions and a 300-metre long water slide. The final weekend a party was held in the closed-off street, which was preceded by a street carnival with an ecomobility theme.

△
Hundreds of exhibition visitors tested small ecomobile vehicles on the test track.

△
The City of Kaohsiung, Taiwan, donated twenty bicycles to share information about their bike-sharing system and announced that they are hosting the next EcoMobility World Festival.

△
A Swedish exhibitor showcases trailers to transport children or goods.

▽
A visitor explores the EcoMobility Expo Online.

▽▽
Children's group learns about transport history and current challenges at the interactive museum "Our History of Transport".

▽
During the last week of the festival, the exhibition was hosted in Alexandra. More than 2,300 children visited and learnt about transport. Many of them learnt how to ride a bike.

△
Johannesburg Mayor Parks Tau is presented with a green helmet by Monika Zimmermann (ICLEI – Local Governments for Sustainability). Along with other city and province officials, he committed to travelling by public transport and cycling during the festival month.

△
View of the Sandton skyline with Gautrain Station and Sandton Public Transport Interchange in the foreground. While Rivonia Road (left, with cars) was opened for car traffic, West Street (right) was closed, and only certain sections were accessible with cars for local users. Access was managed by Johannesburg Metropolitan Police Department officers.

▷The sidewalks along West Street were widened before the festival.

▽▷
A bus from Soweto arrives at the Sandton Gautrain Station. Here, passengers can change to minibus taxi shuttles to reach their workplaces.

▽
Mayors and other city leaders adopted the "Declaration on Ecomobility in Cities" on the final day of the EcoMobility Dialogues.

2 **Changing
the way you move**

"South Africa is a car-centric country and when you start doing something that is related to cars or tempering what motorists do, you enter into a space that is 'holy'. People don't want you to disturb that space. They almost consider the cars as an extended body part.
Now we are coming to these people and asking them to change the way they move. That is very intimidating in its nature, and obviously there is a lot of doubt and questioning. But it is good if people do that, because then you are able to say: there is an alternative, use this alternative, try it."

Sipho Nhlapo, operations manager for mobility and freight, Johannesburg Roads Agency

▷
In the Sandton Public Transport Interchange in the Gautrain Station, travellers can board Gautrain feeder buses and minibus taxis. Gautrain and Metrobus extended their services during the festival.

▷
The managed lanes were set up every morning and evening before the rush hour.

▷
The parking lot of Brightwater Commons Shopping Centre in Randburg was turned into a Park & Ride site during the festival.

▷▷
The closure of one lane of West Street allowed ecomobile travellers to use the full width of the lane.

The burden of congested CBDs

For millions worldwide, the commute to and from their workplace in the city centre is part of their daily lives. The travel between home and workplace becomes a daily nightmare in many places around the world—be it in Los Angeles, Tokyo, Sidney, Jakarta, Lagos, or Mumbai.

CBDs are the economic cores and important nodes of employment of metropolitan regions. Command and control centres of modern service economies are located in these central areas, which host headquarters of international firms, business services, and financial institutions. Apart from a high concentration of retail activity, CBDs can also be places for leisure, culture, and entertainment.

CBDs are usually characterised by a high concentration of workplaces and activities in a small area. Businesses value the face-to-face interaction and efficient flows of information that CBDs offer. Due to these benefits and the high demand for land, these business districts have historically grown vertically rather than horizontally—creating the iconic skylines of cities like New York, Shanghai, and Frankfurt.

When the car emerged as mode of commute, CBDs became gridlocked with cars during peak hours. Endless traffic jams, time-consuming search for parking, and the nuisance of air pollution and noise burden employers and employees, residents, and tourists alike. The benefits of dense agglomeration seemed to perish gradually through the negative effects of traffic congestion.

The consequences of these situations are evident. Businesses that rely on quick and efficient flows of people and goods no longer see themselves able to forecast travel time, plan journeys, and schedule meetings. The attractiveness of the workplace and quality of life are diminished due to the hassle of the daily commute. The non-productive time spent in traffic jams implies an individual, social, and economic loss that is highly significant.

CBDs continue to grow and flourish—despite global trends like the proliferation of modern communication technologies and continuing suburbanisation of people and workplaces. Many city authorities have recognised the advantages of the CBD model and have successfully intervened at the levels of transportation and land-use planning to keep their centres liveable, attractive, and competitive. The CBDs of New York, London, and Tokyo maintain their status as hubs of the world economy. Yet, the dominance of the automobile in CBDs persists.

Cities in countries with a quickly growing economy in the global south have to deal with population growth, spatial pressure, and social inequalities. In the globally connected business districts of São Paulo, Johannesburg, and Mumbai, the consequences of rapid economic development have become effective and visible. These places need urgent and profound solutions; at the same time, however, they have the chance to act as breeding grounds for social and technological innovations, as arenas for unconventional experimentation. City leaders in industrialised countries should take a closer look at the innovations and experiments that emerge from the new world cities in the global south.

▽
Traffic during rush hour in Chicago

Downtown congestion in cities in the United States

Cities in the United States are the best examples of the severe impacts of car dependency. They are among those with the lowest density in the world. Although new economic hubs have emerged in the suburbs, the economic hotspots have often remained in the downtown area, the historic core of the cities. Every day, millions of cars enter the geographically small central areas from the suburbs. In low-density cities like Atlanta, Houston, Denver, and Phoenix, each individual consumes three to over five times as much energy for transport than an individual in Europe, and multiple times the energy that a commuter in Mumbai or Hong Kong uses. Accordingly, the transport-related CO_2 emissions and pollution levels are very high there.

With carpooling remaining a marginal phenomenon, single-occupancy vehicles clog the motorways each morning and evening. In 2014, car drivers in the US wasted nearly seven billion extra hours and burned over three billion gallons of fuel while sitting in traffic jams. Per commuter, this means an additional forty-two hours and USD 960 for fuel each year. In the most congested cities of the US—including Washington, DC; Los Angeles; San Francisco; and New York—the amount of extra hours rises to eighty each year.

Most US cities have initiated serious measures to improve public transport and infrastructure for walking and cycling. However, the problems arising from the spatial structure of car-oriented cities and the associated mobility habits remain unsolved.

The Gurgaon experience

"Gurgaon is similar to Sandton. Gurgaon is the IT hub in the National Capital Region of India and the biggest GDP producer of Haryana State. Although 35 per cent of the people in Gurgaon are walking or cycling, we don't have 1 per cent of safe infrastructure for them. Decision-makers never plan for pedestrians and cyclists because they all use cars. But the city cannot be a car-centric city; it has to be a people-centric city!

Thus we started an initiative called Raahgiri Day—Open Streets Day—to demonstrate the demand for pedestrian and cycling infrastructure. Every Tuesday on-street parking is prohibited in the major IT corridor of Gurgaon. We work closely with the municipality and the traffic police department.

The police strictly enforce this, the schools embrace it, the top CEOs support it, and the commuters' response has been excellent. They use the metro system, auto rickshaws, carpooling, and the new shuttle bus services.

After Raahgiri and CarFreeDay, the authority is prioritising public transport and non-motorised transport infrastructure. A first cycle track has been implemented, and new street designs with cycle tracks, walkways, zones for street vendors, and green areas will be implemented. It is amazing to see that result in Gurgaon!"

Sarika Panda-Bhatt, manager, cities and transport, World Resources Institute, India

"We risk Sandton becoming a big parking lot"

Sandton CBD, the economic hub of South Africa, experiences an influx of 120,000 commuters and over 75,000 cars daily. During the morning and evening rush periods, Sandton is usually gridlocked, with traffic jams on all major access roads to Sandton. For those who incur the daily commute by car in peak hours, travel times have become unpredictable. Commuting becomes a stressful and time-intensive daily necessity. Although some commuters have developed strategies to avoid the peak traffic—for instance, by leaving from home early in the morning or working until late in the office—Sandton's rush-hour traffic remains unbearable.

The high volumes of traffic and the congestion not only affect the vehicle drivers, but rising noise and pollution levels also affect the surrounding residential neighbourhoods. Frustration behind the wheel and speeding drivers lead to accidents often involving those who are not protected by the steel cage of the automobile—the pedestrians. Full streets force buses and minibuses to move slowly. Bus commuters spend up to three hours in the bus for a one-way journey—for example, to reach Sandton from southern Soweto—not only due to distance, but also due to traffic jams. This means that those who already use public transport—and contribute the least to congestion—also experience the major burden of congestion.

The province of Gauteng is currently experiencing massive migration from other parts of South Africa and neighbouring countries. According to estimates, the province's population could double in the next two to three decades, leading to an enormous increase in the number of vehicles. Research shows that twenty-five years from now, the average vehicle speed at peak hours in Gauteng will be fifteen kilometres per hour. Ismail Vadi, member of the executive council (MEC) for roads and transport of the Province of Gauteng, concludes: "In your BMW, you will actually be moving slower than a horse or a cart."

Additionally, Sandton currently is being densified by new high-rise buildings, some of them replacing smaller buildings not even three decades old. Real estate developers try to deal with the projected demand for parking spaces by building increasingly larger parking garages below their office towers. However, the capacity of Sandton's streets to carry additional traffic is exhausted. Even today, 89 per cent of Sandton's commuters feel affected by congestion. "We risk Sandton becoming a big parking lot", says Mayor Parks Tau.

"Sandton is a very important economic space. However, if you cannot get in and out of Sandton, ultimately people will leave Sandton and there will be less of a capacity to have this agglomeration of people being able to contribute to the economy. So it is very important to make Sandton function."

Lisa Seftel, executive director for transport,
City of Johannesburg

"I have seen a lot of changes in Sandton. When Sandton City Mall was built, some people came on horseback to the shopping centre. The area was not designed for the daily commute of so many people. Also in the library we feel this change, less people come nowadays. I think it is due to the difficult accessibility. If you are stuck in traffic so long to reach the library, it is not worth coming."

Margaret Houliston, manager, Sandton Library

Where do Sandton's employees come from?

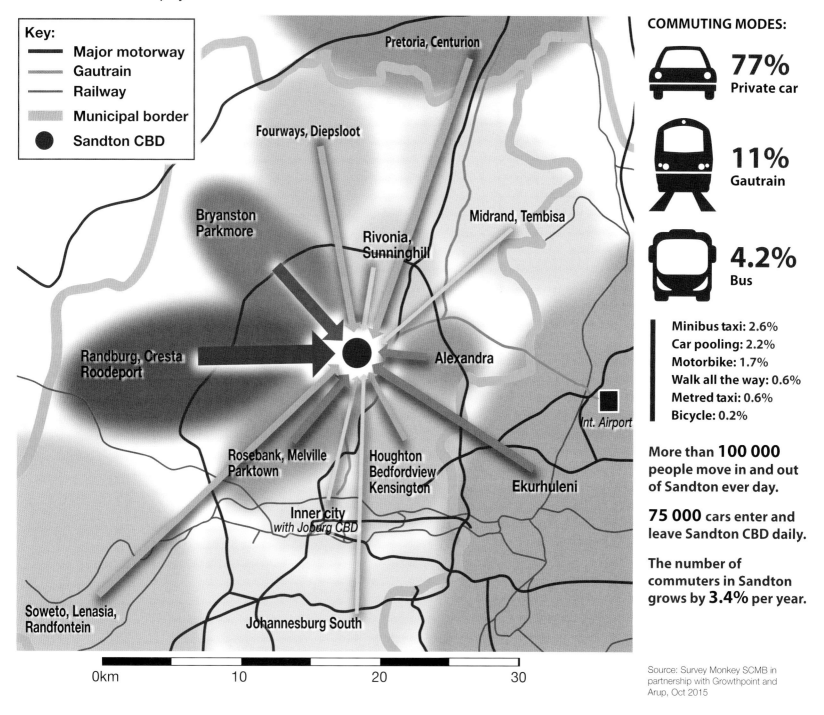

Key:
- ▬▬ Major motorway
- ▬▬ Gautrain
- —— Railway
- ▓▓ Municipal border
- ● Sandton CBD

Pretoria, Centurion

Fourways, Diepsloot

Bryanston Parkmore

Rivonia, Sunninghill

Midrand, Tembisa

Randburg, Cresta Roodeport

Alexandra

Int. Airport

Rosebank, Melville Parktown

Houghton Bedfordview Kensington

Ekurhuleni

Inner city *with Joburg CBD*

Soweto, Lenasia, Randfontein

Johannesburg South

0km   10   20   30

COMMUTING MODES:

77% Private car

11% Gautrain

4.2% Bus

Minibus taxi: 2.6%
Car pooling: 2.2%
Motorbike: 1.7%
Walk all the way: 0.6%
Metred taxi: 0.6%
Bicycle: 0.2%

More than **100 000** people move in and out of Sandton ever day.

75 000 cars enter and leave Sandton CBD daily.

The number of commuters in Sandton grows by **3.4%** per year.

Source: Survey Monkey SCMB in partnership with Growthpoint and Arup, Oct 2015

27

"The traffic bothers me every day": Zanele's commute by car to Sandton

Zanele and her family live in a northern suburb of Johannesburg, around six kilometres away from Sandton. She and her family live in a gated community, a form of fenced-off residential neighbourhood that is typical to Johannesburg's northern suburbs. Both Zanele and her husband study, work, and go to the same gym in Sandton.

Mode of commute:	car
Distance to Sandton:	6 kilometres
Travel time:	30–40 minutes
Travel speed:	9–12 km kilometres/hour
Cost:	R 10 fuel + R 18 parking + additional costs

Around 8 a.m., they both leave for Sandton, however, in different cars. Driving through the neighbourhood, she explains: "He might have things to do in the afternoon and I might want to go somewhere else. We like the freedom of it."

The skyline of Sandton appears on the horizon. "Since I have a car, I never used public transport again." Zanele approaches Sandton Drive, one of the arterial roads leading into Sandton. "Look at the traffic! Can you imagine this every single morning? It is insane!"

She drives up Fifth Street and notices the construction work: "Within Sandton, all cars have to fit in two lanes only. If more people work and live here, you need more road space." She enters a parking garage. "I pay 180 rand per week for parking. That is a lot of money!"

"Once I saw a man cycling on my route. It took him the same time, so I thought it is possible to cycle. There are no showers in the library, but I could cycle to the gym, take a shower there and have a nice stroll to the library."

"In South Africa, we are very attached to our cars. When we get our first jobs, we want to buy a car. But we are very stressed drivers because we spend so much time in traffic. I have lived in Johannesburg for twenty years and I never walked. But I want to be outside, I wish I could walk around Sandton. It would be so nice to walk, meet people, chat, and feel like you live in a city.

I would use public transport if it were more convenient, frequent, and safe. I was very happy to see the cycle lanes coming up for the festival. I regularly run in the gym—so why not just cycle or run to Sandton instead? I could easily cycle the distance from my home if it were safer. I wish they would put cycle lanes everywhere."

Moving inside Sandton: last-mile (dis)connection

Car commuting to and from Sandton is congesting the arterial roads around and within Sandton. In and around the CBD, cars and the more recently introduced three-wheeler taxis—so-called tuk-tuks—are also used for short-distance trips, producing additional amounts of automobile traffic.

Sandton was not designed as a CBD, but developed without a proper plan. As it grew in size and importance, the layout of the district was adapted to accommodate the growing number of private vehicles. Wide thoroughfares and multi-storey parking garages provide car users with convenient access to workplaces and shopping centres. Priority was given to the automobile, and infrastructure for walking and cycling received less attention. Thus, the absence or poor shape of infrastructure for pedestrians and cyclists discourages those who are able to make a choice between automobile and ecomobile travel.

Yet, a significant number of employees and visitors travel to Sandton by public transport, including by minibus taxis, and many walk to their workplaces—mainly from the township of Alexandra. Everyone who uses ecomobile forms of travel to Sandton also needs to walk and cycle within Sandton, whether it is for the last-mile connection from the bus stop to the workplace or for a lunch break on the other side of the street. Narrow sidewalks, dark corners next to wide entrances of parking garages, and reckless driving behaviour make the walking experience unpleasant. A network of privately owned tunnels and bridges connects many of the malls and office towers, and people would rather use the indoor walkways than cross the streets. Hence, for many of those who arrive in parking garages by car, this essentially means never stepping out on the street at all during the entire day.

"Even though I live on Grayston Drive, which is very close to Sandton CBD, I commute by car. Only in the car I feel safe. People need to have confidence about their safety. When I am afraid and don't feel safe, I don't walk. The City needs to put more security and police patrol on the streets."

Rhidima, works at a merchandise company in Sandton

Ecomobilising Sandton: the festival approach

The City of Johannesburg developed an ambitious Transport Management Plan for the festival month. This plan was designed to offer an integrated system that comprises various travel options to and from Sandton, as well as the last-mile connection within the CBD. For one month, the citizens of Johannesburg could experience what a future comprehensive transport system based on the principles of ecomobility could look like, and that it could be safe, comfortable, reliable, and environmentally friendly.

Johannesburg had already been promoting sustainable transport through its planning and policies for many years. The Managed Lanes Policy of 2012, the Complete Streets Policy of 2013, and the Non-Motorised Transport Framework are examples of these efforts; all of them demonstrate a major paradigm shift away from car-centric urban development.

The establishment of the Gautrain in 2010 has set a new standard for transport in South Africa. Modern high-speed trains link Sandton to the Johannesburg CBD, Pretoria, and the OR Tambo International Airport, as well as other major business centres along the route. A feeder bus system provides access from residential neighbourhoods to the rail system. Since its introduction, thousands of frustrated car users have embraced the new alternative and changed their everyday commute. In Johannesburg alone, the total patronage of the system has increased to a monthly ridership of 857,000 in October 2015. With more than 300,000 monthly passengers, Sandton is the busiest Gautrain station in Johannesburg. Although the Gautrain has become very popular, ticket prices are fairly high and large segments of the population cannot afford it as mode of daily commute.

Although a necessity for those who cannot afford cars, walking and cycling are increasingly being recognised as part of a healthy and eco-friendly lifestyle in urban South Africa. Thus, the EcoMobility World Festival 2015 came at the right time to experiment with addressing those who are often considered to be "unteachable": the aspiring urban middle classes with great affinity to cars. But instead of imposing a mode of travel, the approach is to change the minds and behaviours of car users by providing the opportunity to experience the alternatives. The festival offered a perfect framework for urging citizens to "change the way they move".

Components for moving to and from Sandton

Managed lanes

Park & Ride facilities

Cycling routes

Public transport services

The festival's Transport Management Plan for Sandton

The comprehensive Transport Management Plan encouraged people to "change the way they move". Instead of prohibiting car use in the business district of Sandton, the plan aimed instead at creating discomfort for private car users while travelling to or inside Sandton. While this should stimulate a change towards using alternative transport modes, the operability of South Africa's most dynamic economic hub needed to be secured. For deliveries and all those who saw themselves unable to use the provided alternatives, access by car users to all buildings was maintained over the month.

The results of previously conducted studies—such as the Sandton Transport Plan and the study for the future alignment of the extension of the bus rapid transit system Rea Vaya—were included in the plan. Furthermore, the businesses of Sandton were asked to provide information about how many employees come to Sandton by car and from where they commute, in order to determine suitable Park & Ride sites and additional public transport offers.

The creation of the Transport Management Plan took several months. Property owners, tenants, and residents of the CBD were invited to take part in the formulation of the plan in several stakeholder meetings and more than eighty consultations with single actors in Sandton. The final version of the plan finds an appropriate balance between the visions of the city administration and the requirements of Sandton's business and residential communities. The process and the outcome stand for fostering long-term sustainable development that does not exclude certain actors, but benefits everyone.

"In the future, if you want to sit in traffic for two and a half hours in peak time, if that is the lifestyle you choose, then stay in a car. But if you want to be more efficient, better organised in life, and have more quality time with your family, then you have to look at either public transport or other modes of non-motorised transport."

Ismail Vadi, MEC for roads and transport, Province of Gauteng

Components for moving within Sandton

Priority to ecomobility ("Festival Footprint")

Last-mile services

Public transport loop

Traffic flow control

Moving in Sandton: the Festival Footprint

The EcoMobility Festival Footprint determined those areas where ecomobility was given priority over private, motorised vehicles. On Rivonia Road, Fredman Drive and Fifth Street, one street lane was dedicated to public transport services, and a shuttle service ran in an anticlockwise loop. This lane was closed to private vehicles, and access for authorised owners and residents was managed by Johannesburg Metro Police Department officers. This loop also delimited the festival area.

In this precinct, car movement was limited on Alice Lane, Maude Street, Gwen Lane, Stella Street, and West Street. Through-traffic was inhibited by closing access from Alice Lane and Maude Street into West Street. To further discourage the use of cars in Sandton's central alley, West Street was narrowed to one lane for each direction. The remaining traffic comprised only local users and construction vehicles.

The western lane of West Street became the main ecomobile boulevard, accessible only to pedestrians, non-motorised vehicles, and small electric vehicles. For the convenience of pedestrians and cyclists, the sidewalk on West Street was permanently widened, and a new cycle path created. As part of the cycle track to Alexandra, a pop-up bicycle lane with cones and signage was implemented on Maude Street. Access was permitted to all buildings and construction sites, ensuring that business operation, deliveries, and construction could continue as usual. Traffic control personnel were deployed at six managed access points, to ensure that only those users could enter certain streets that needed to access adjacent buildings.

> "I've been in Sandton before, traffic is crazy. This time it's more pleasant; you find things that help you to use the space without cars, like the exhibition or tuk-tuks that take you around."
>
> Nick and Christal, Sandton visitors

△▽
The loop service distributed passengers from the Gautrain station, the bus stops, and Park & Ride shuttle bus stops to their destinations in Sandton. It used a street lane that was restricted to the use of public transport services. There were eight stops along the route. The service was offered free of charge with a five-minute frequency during peak hours.

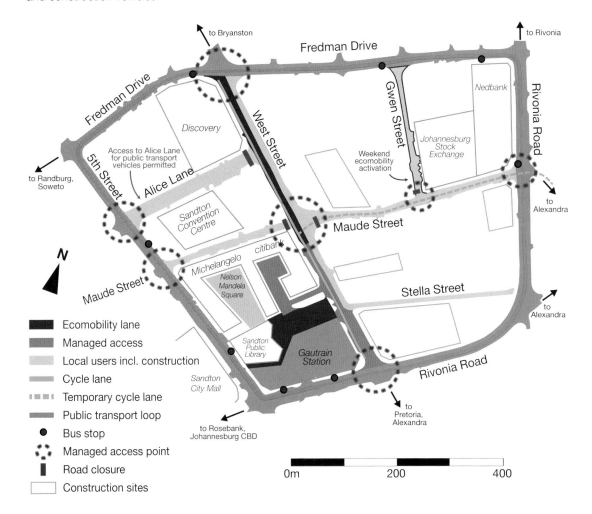

Legend:
- Ecomobility lane
- Managed access
- Local users incl. construction
- Cycle lane
- Temporary cycle lane
- Public transport loop
- ● Bus stop
- Managed access point
- Road closure
- □ Construction sites

0m   200   400

Smart solutions for the last mile

Distances to the next public transport station are sometimes longer than people prefer to walk. Also during the festival period, people needed to reach their offices from the Gautrain station or a shuttle bus drop-off point. A lot of small ecomobile vehicles exist, which can make this "last mile" more comfortable and allow new social business concepts or sharing models.

"At the interchange point Park Station, people change modes from buses to trains, metred taxis, or minibus taxis. But there is no formal way of distributing the people locally. Everybody who gets there has to walk.
Hence we are looking into other options, like pedicabs, to make sure that we distribute the people through real integrated public transport, covering the last mile to office or home as well."
Phumlani N. Mngomezulu, entrepreneur, MD–Blacodo Holdings (Pty) Ltd

Apart from ecomobile vehicles for short passenger trips, the delivery of goods and services produces substantial traffic in dense areas like CBDs. The festival also encouraged entrepreneurs to present innovative, ecomobile provision of goods and services.

"GezaJozi is a social enterprise that equips informal waste collectors with a Geza Tryke. We empower the recyclists by giving them this tricycle, which is safer and more efficient on the road. At the festival, we are driving around, sorting out the food stands, and collecting waste where it is."
Gabriel, GezaJozi

The EcoMobility World Exhibition presented several innovative ecomobile vehicles. While they are becoming increasingly popular, regulation, licensing, and certification of these vehicles is yet unresolved in South Africa and many other countries. During the festival, this hurdle also prevented manufacturers and service operators from offering more types of ecomobile last-mile services.

"Our regulatory system does not allow these types of vehicles on our roads. During the EcoMobility World Festival, we could use these vehicles in places where we aren't usually allowed to do so. For instance, we were running Segway tours around Sandton, and people loved them.
Hopefully this festival is going to ignite our government to look at our legislation and start putting infrastructure in place that will support new mobility products, so that people can integrate them into their lifestyles and use them for everyday travel. This is the creation of a tipping point where green mobility can finally enter South Africa."
Jonathan Cohen, managing director, Imperial Green Mobility

Moving to and from Sandton: integrated public transport

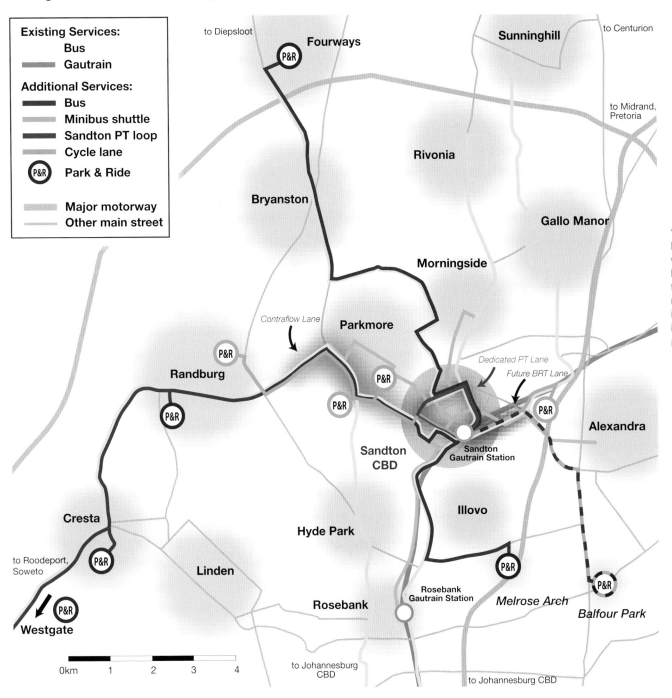

Existing Services:
- Bus
- Gautrain

Additional Services:
- Bus
- Minibus shuttle
- Sandton PT loop
- Cycle lane
- P&R Park & Ride

- Major motorway
- Other main street

to Diepsloot

Fourways
P&R

Sunninghill
to Centurion

to Midrand, Pretoria

Rivonia

Bryanston

Gallo Manor

Morningside

Contraflow Lane

Parkmore

Dedicated PT Lane
Future BRT Lane

Randburg
P&R

P&R

P&R

P&R

Alexandra

Sandton CBD

Sandton Gautrain Station

Cresta

Illovo

Hyde Park

to Roodeport, Soweto
P&R

Linden

Rosebank Gautrain Station

P&R

Melrose Arch

Balfour Park
P&R

P&R
Westgate

Rosebank

0km 1 2 3 4

to Johannesburg CBD

to Johannesburg CBD

"Instead of using my car, I commute by bus for the whole festival month. It is a lot cheaper because I save the fuel. The bus is more relaxed, as driving the car is very stressful when there is heavy traffic."

Kaiser, works in a bank in Sandton

11 Park & Ride facilities
6 additional bus shuttles
5 additional van shuttles
4 additional cycling routes

Additional buses and extended Gautrain services

Due to their importance as commuting alternatives, the services of the Gautrain played a major role in the festival's transport management. Gautrain supported the festival by increasing the train frequency on weekends from two to three trains per hour, and the extension of the afternoon peak period on weekdays.

Metrobus—the municipal bus company—and the private operator Putco provided additional bus services from major commuting origins into Sandton. Gautrain ran a non-stop express bus service from one Park & Ride location. Furthermore, the minibus taxi industry was contracted to run free shuttle buses from Park & Ride sites into the Sandton CBD (see map) and around a public transport loop. On two of the congested major access roads into Sandton, dedicated public transport lanes allowed all collective transport services to bypass car traffic.

"I have been using the Gautrain and the Gautrain bus from its beginning. Before, I commuted by car for twenty years. The change was easy as it has only benefits: I save fuel, I don't need to change the tires of my car that often, and the best thing is that I am not frustrated when I arrive at work in the morning. I couldn't stand all that frustration from being stuck in traffic anymore."

Rebecca, office worker in Sandton

"I have never been on a bus before"

"I live in Cresta and work for a bank in Sandton. I have been commuting by car for five years, and I have seen the traffic in Sandton getting worse and worse every day. I moved closer to Sandton because I hated commuting. The EcoMobility Festival suits me perfectly. The Park & Ride spot is quite close to my home!

During the festival, I am using the Putco bus from the Park & Ride in Cresta to Sandton. I have never been on a bus before! I walk three kilometres to the shopping mall where the Park & Ride is located. The walk to the bus stop is nice, the bus stop is easy to find, the people there are very helpful, and it is well organised. I will maintain it for the whole month. I am really happy, and I think it is the right thing to do. I see the walking as an exercise. You meet new people on the bus, and everyone who is doing it is excited. There is a lady working in my office, whom I never talked to before. This morning we were sitting in the same bus and we were chatting. Furthermore, I recently started an online training, so I use the time on the bus to watch videos. Choosing Sandton as location for this festival is quite a big statement. It makes the problems visible, highlights changes that are necessary, and forces people to be part of the change."

Sarah, works in a bank in Sandton

Park & Ride facilities

In order to reduce vehicular trips to Sandton CBD, ten Park & Ride sites were installed during the festival. Some of them were located in the vicinity of Sandton next to the residential neighbourhoods. These sites were served by free minibus taxi shuttles, which brought commuters directly into the heart of Sandton. Other Park & Ride services were located in different northern and western suburbs of Johannesburg, where many of the car commuters live. Bus services, including non-stop express buses, provided a convenient link between these facilities and the Sandton CBD.

The Park & Rides were operating within the morning and evening peak periods from 6 a.m. to 9 a.m. and from 3.30 p.m. to 6 p.m. free of cost. The Park & Ride appealed to commuters in numerous ways. Because several sites were located next to residential areas, commuters just walked there and used the transport services, not driving their cars at all. Nevertheless, the Park & Ride sites were not used by car commuters as much as the City had envisioned.

Managed lanes

To encourage the use of public transport services from the outlying areas of Johannesburg to Sandton, some bottleneck corridors were identified that could feasibly be "bypassed" by public transport to create a meaningful passenger time-saver compared to private car trips.

Contraflow lanes for peak-direction public transport were temporarily installed on Republic Road, along William Nicol Drive, and on Sandton Drive. These lanes were taken from the respective off-peak direction lane. The future BRT lane along Katherine Street was utilised as a with-flow lane. The managed lanes were demarcated with traffic cones and temporary signage. Traffic officers were deployed to all junctions to ensure smooth operations. They overrode the traffic signals to give public transport priority at intersections and to provide safety for all road users and pedestrians.

For four weeks, this unprecedented logistical effort allowed public transport commuters to bypass notorious traffic congestion in peak hours and reach their workplace or home safely, relaxed, and in less time. Public transport users reduced their daily commute by up to thirty minutes.

△
From the Gautrain station and other stops around the public transport loop, express buses and minibus taxi shuttles departed to the Park & Ride sites.

▽
Buses as well as minibus taxis were allowed to use the managed lanes.

Temporary cycle routes and dedicated cycle lanes

In order to encourage cycling as a mode of daily transport, four cycling routes to Sandton CBD were demarcated:

On the **Eastern Route from Alexandra**, a bicycle track with separate signalling was implemented to provide a safer and faster alternative for the 10,000 daily pedestrians between Alexandra and Sandton. A complementing cycle and pedestrian bridge over the M1 motorway is under construction.

The **Northern and Western Routes** pass through residential neighbourhoods to encourage car commuters to shift to cycling.

The **Southern Route** connected the two major commercial and business hubs, Rosebank and Sandton. On this heavily congested route, the cycle path encourages frequent business travellers to cycle to work.

Johannesburg through the eyes of cyclists

"When I grew up, my identity was fused with my motorcar. Then I started doing short rides and discovered how great it is to experience the city more immediately. You arrive at your destination more relaxed, more in touch, more grounded. I haven't yet got rid of my car completely, but with the mix of public transport, Uber taxis, and cycling, it is almost possible now. I believe that we cyclists have as much right to be on the road as someone driving a car—and we take up less space! The best way to make cycling safer in Johannesburg would be for more people to ride a bike!
There has been the perception that cycling is a white, middle-class, recreational activity. But if you look at who is taking trips throughout the day on bikes, it is black working-class commuters. This is important in terms of planning."

Crispian Olver, Cycle Jozi Forum

"Cycling makes absolute sense to me. It is basically free; you are in control of your own destiny and get wind in your hair.
People on bicycles create democratic spaces. No one is using more space than the other, no matter how expensive the bike is. Also you can engage with the other person quite easily. Being together on the road, you identify with one another."

David Du Preez, Johannesburg Urban Cyclists Association (JUCA)

"I cycle to work daily and to meetings in Sandton, Rosebank, and/or the inner city. Often I am faster than my colleagues who drive cars, partly because of the traffic and partly because of the parking situation. I can park the bicycle right in front of the building.
It is important to improve the cycling infrastructure and to provide subsidies for people to help them buy bicycles. Affordability is critical in getting more people on bikes."

Adrian Enthoven, chairman, Hollard Insurance Company Ltd

Planning the change, changing the plans

Vuyiswa Tlomatsane and Adrian Brislin, transport planners from the consulting firm MPA Investment, were in charge of preparing the Transport Management Plan (TMP) for the festival.

Planning the commute of 100,000 people is a big task. How did you proceed to set up the TMP?

MPA We started to work on it just four months before the festival started. We defined the public transport loop, which became the perimeter of the Festival Footprint. Then we had consultations with the companies within this area to determine the transport requirements of their employees.

The more detailed the plan became, the more anxiety the corporate side revealed about how their thousands of employees could access their buildings. Due to the negotiations between the City and the stakeholders, the Festival Footprint changed substantially—literally on a daily basis.

Even during the festival, the plan was not static. We were constantly evaluating the situation and making improvements. For example, we discontinued certain Park & Ride sites due to poor usage and improved public transport services in other areas.

How did you approach the people who commute by car?

MPA For most car commuters, saving time is more important than saving money. Hence, we used time-saving as an incentive for people to change their mode of transport.

Based on the information from the companies about the origins of their employees, we identified suitable Park & Ride sites. In order to realise lower travel times for those who switched to public transport, we installed dedicated public transport lanes. Otherwise, the buses and minibus taxis would also be stuck in traffic.

So people from all over Johannesburg could park their cars and come by bus?

MPA We served those who enter Sandton from the west and the north very well. The biggest challenge during the festival was for the 29 per cent of commuters from the south of Johannesburg—for example, Soweto. Public transport services from there are not sufficient, and the routes are heavily congested. Unless there is a public transport priority lane, there is no time benefit.

What were the biggest challenges in implementing the TMP?

MPA Originally, we thought about a much larger system of dedicated public transport lanes, but as the safety management of the lanes is extremely manpower intensive and needs constant monitoring, we had to reduce the extent. Another challenge was to get the bus and minibus taxi drivers to understand how the TMP works around Sandton and which diversions they have to take. We met on a weekly basis to discuss the system, to conduct training, and to have dry runs. Nonetheless, some buses got stuck on the first day.

The third challenge was the communication with the public. We had a lot of queries each day from people who did not know how they would be affected. This was very time-consuming.

What will remain from the festival month?

MPA Although not as many people have switched to the provided alternatives as we had hoped, for us the outcome is great: because for those who did change, they did it of their own will and not because they were forced. Most people who used the system were very excited about it!

"The movement will start here and it will spread across the country"

Sipho Nhlapo (SN) is the operations manager for mobility and freight of the Johannesburg Roads Agency.

Why would people change their behaviour?

SN Interestingly, a lot of South Africans who get to travel abroad are quick to tell you: "I cycled in Germany, it was so nice. I jumped into public transport in London, it was so nice." When they come back to South Africa, we want them to forget about their car keys and travel by public transport.

People in Sandton have a choice—they can actually choose to switch and to park their cars in the Park & Ride for at least that one month.

As organisers of the festival, we needed to overcome fear. I think we have managed to do so, but we still had to make people excited about the change. Many people say they would change, but there is no proper alternative.

People tend to say there is no public transport in Johannesburg. I have got a different opinion. I think there is public transport; it is just not attractive. It is not the kind of transport that people want to jump on to. In Johannesburg, more than 48 per cent of 1.5 million daily trips are made using public transport.

Where is the problem then?

SN Public transport is not cool yet. A car is considered a cool thing to have. For a lot of young people, they will get into private cars as soon as they have enough money. Thus, we need to find ways of making public transport a cool and nice mode to use. It is there and it is moving a lot of people. We just need to make it attractive, so that each and every person can use it and find comfort in it.

Safety is one of car commuters' prime concerns. How can this be dealt with?

SN It is difficult for people to trust taxis if these don't abide by the rules of the road. It is difficult when people occasionally see one of our buses involved in an accident. And people quickly say: "See, it is not safe". People bring up the safety issue all the time. But we know the safety numbers. If people cycle together in a cycle train, they feel safer. If people walk in a group, they will feel safer. If people walk a lot in the street and more of them are in the street, they feel safer. But if people don't do that, they will not feel safer.

Why is Sandton the right place for the festival?

SN Sandton is a very sensitive space. If people in Sandton can do it, we know that it can be done everywhere in this country. If we had done it in a very quiet place, people would not know about it. The movement will start here and spread across the country, and we will be happy about it.

"I do believe that you can change people's mind by changing your own behaviour. You show leadership, you must be willing to make sacrifices."
Christine Walters, MMC for transport, City of Johannesburg

"It is important that leaders are not just preaching messages, but actually doing it in their daily lives."
Prof. Philip Harrison, University of the Witwatersrand, Johannesburg

▽
A large awareness and activation campaign informed commuters in Sandton and other parts of Johannesburg about the different commuting options during the festival.

3

Stitching the
city together

"We are restitching our city to create a different future for our residents, where we can link jobs to people and people to jobs."

Mpho Parks Tau, executive mayor,
City of Johannesburg

"So what we are going to do is unite our community through transport and through transport infrastructure."

Christine Walters, MMC for transport,
City of Johannesburg

▷
The Streets Alive parade linked Sandton to Alexandra on the opening day of the festival.

▷
The minibus taxi industry, provider of transport services to remote townships, was a festival partner.

▷
The City partnered with Qhubeka, the World Bicycle Relief's programme in South Africa. Through this programme, specially designed and locally assembled bicycles are distributed to people in need. Bicycle Empowerment Centres, like this one in Soweto, provide training and empower communities.

▷▷
4,000 cyclists joined the Freedom Ride, among them local political leaders and children.

Socio-spatial divide in urban regions

Social and economic differences between population groups exist in every urban society. However, in the second half of the last century, income inequality has increased all over the world. While inequality is drastically rising in parts of Asia, the highest inequality levels are found in Africa and Latin America. Inequality is not just associated with poverty and differences in income, but also with different living standards, access to resources and basic services, and varying opportunities in taking part in social and political life. As the number of people living in urban areas is increasing worldwide, cities are the places where extreme social and economic disparities become visible, sometimes leading to social unrest or conflicts.

Inequality is often connected to a spatial dimension and mobility. Historically, people of higher economic status tended to live together in the same neighbourhoods. The process of suburbanisation—the movement out of the city by the middle classes—was made possible first by the railway and later by the private car. Residential suburbanisation was often succeeded by a shift of businesses and services to the outskirts. Those with poor access to jobs, housing, and transport remained in the inner city. In some countries, economic segregation is paired with racial or ethnic segregation, as in the US and South Africa, where spatial segregation was part of a political and legal system.

The low-density middle-class neighbourhoods outside city limits are only one form of spatial segregation. With increasing revalorisation of inner-city life among the affluent, poor and rich often live next to each other in cities, yet are completely separated by the walls and security fences of gated communities. This relatively new phenomenon is a challenge for policymakers and planners in both developed and developing countries.

Inequality that takes a spatial effect is a particular challenge in terms of providing comprehensive and high-quality public transport services to every urban citizen. In low-density areas, public transport has a hard time competing with

△
In Mumbai, high-rise luxury apartments are often developed next to slums and squatter settlements.

private vehicles. In high-density areas with a large portion of people living in poverty, transport services are still of poor quality in many cities. Unattractive to those who can afford different means of transport, the spatial separation of economic classes is then perpetuated in different transport options. The vicious circle of income inequality, spatial separation, and the failure of the market to provide high-quality services to low-income citizens can only be broken by strong state intervention.

◁
Car-centric development has contributed to low-density suburbanisation, also called "urban sprawl".

"We have to agree on the vision of the city that we want"

"Mexico City had the same problems with safety in the streets and the safety of mobility as Johannesburg. Mexico City's society is very polarised—we have a lot of people from different origins and with different incomes. It's a very classist society. We have to fight for an equal society, we have to work to reunite and to take care of everyone. We still don't have the city that we are trying to make, but we are working on it.
Any society needs to know that motorised mobility is not going to be the solution for the future. And people need to know that ecomobility has to be a priority for all to have safe, comfortable, and cheap mobility. Ecomobility is a way of transforming the city, a way to get a safer and more secure city, a way to get jobs. We have to agree on the vision of the city that we want as a society. If we don't have the same vision, it is going to be very difficult.
The rise of the bicycle in Mexico City has been an amazing experience. No one thought cycling would be possible, especially not as a means of transport. Then we started with the Open Street Programme ten years ago. That was a key to getting people on the bikes. Although it was on Sundays, people got the chance to take over a safe environment and to experience riding a bicycle in the street. Nowadays, we see lots of cyclists. This development shows the hope and ambition of Mexico City and Mexican society."

Iván De La Lanza Gámiz, design, culture and bicycle infrastructure director, Mexico City, Mexico

"Although so many people walk, the facilities are in a bad state"

"The big differences that I see between Sandton and Alexandra, we also have in Kampala. There is a very big slum about two-and-a-half kilometres from an upscale area, where the State House, the President's seat, is located. There are the huge businesses, the hotels, the opportunities for poor people to find casual work. In Kampala, poor people walk because they have no other choice, so they tend to live close to their workplaces in the city centre; 60 per cent of people are walking, a few are cycling. Although so many people walk, the facilities for pedestrians are in a bad state.
If you are poor, it means you are going to spend a lot of money on things like health and education. If the poor person has to pay much for everything, it is like hitting them with a nail in the head. They cannot develop. If public transport were less expensive, they could at least save some money on transport costs.
People want to move and everybody has a right to move, so we have to find ways to reduce the costs of movement—this is valid for the poor and the rich alike. Ecomobility for poor people is about not feeling condemned for being poor. Ecomobility for the wealthier should not condemn them for being rich. I understand ecomobility as a very broad concept because in the long run it is going to affect the economic well-being and the social well-being of the city."

Amanda Ngabirano Aziidah, Makerere University, Kampala, Uganda

The legacy of apartheid planning: inscribed in space, perpetuated in mobility

Johannesburg shares its socio-spatial problems with many of the world's large cities. However, the very particular history of being built on a legally sanctioned system of separation makes Johannesburg's contemporary challenges unique among world cities.

South African cities have been shaped in the deliberate attempt to separate people from each other by race. Especially in Johannesburg, the divide is deeply inscribed in the history of the city. Its origins as a mining town are linked to the exploitation and control of workers from black communities by colonial powers and white industrialists. Hundred years of marginalisation and neglect—including forty-six years of apartheid as political programme—have disadvantaged the non-white communities to an extent that after more than twenty years of democracy, the racial divides are still evident and the economic inequalities are rising.

One of the reasons the divides continue to play a role in the lives of the majority is that apartheid has effectively cast the separation in stone, steel, and concrete. The 1913 Land Act legalised evictions of Africans from their homes, and the Native Urban Areas Act of 1923 gave authorities the power to establish separate living areas for Africans, usually at the edges of the city. When the black urban population increased substantially in the nineteen-forties, the government responded by passing laws that aimed at controlling all aspects of Africans' lives. Among these laws, the Group Areas Act of 1950 had the most significant spatial consequences. Seeking strict residential segregation along race, every town and city was divided into areas that were reserved for one race only. Africans were forcibly removed from inner-city locations and brought to dedicated townships far away from the centre. Public infrastructure— and especially transport—also became strictly segregated.

After the liberation from apartheid, the core city and the townships around were administratively integrated into the City of Johannesburg. While new densely built-up economic hubs like Sandton evolved north of the Johannesburg CBD in the wealthy low-density suburbs, job creation close to the townships did not pick up significantly. Today, Johannesburg is one of the largest cities in the world in terms of area size, and among those with the lowest population density. Apartheid's spatial system resulted in residential areas with the lowest density being closest to income opportunities, and high-density townships remaining far away. This very unique fact is an extraordinary challenge for planners and policymakers.

For those living in the townships, still predominantly the African communities, distances to their jobs are enormous. The public transport system, especially the railway system, which originated in the apartheid era, does not cater to these communities by giving them access to jobs in the sprawling economic centres of north Johannesburg. Instead, an informal system of minibus taxis predominantly provides these services, and they were often perceived as unsafe and costly. Large distances and poor transport options result in longer commuting times (average fifty-six minutes) for black South Africans in the Gauteng region, compared to white South Africans (average forty-two minutes).

With the continuing influx of migrants, older, dense residential neighbourhoods are becoming increasingly densely populated. Those who can afford it, seek to escape the dense townships into the townships extensions, which are relatively low in density. For wealthy citizens, low-density gated communities far outside the core have become attractive. This ongoing development—from spatial segregation based on race into segregation along economic classes—poses a particular challenge to the goal of comprehensive transit coverage.

The distance on the road from Orange Farm, the southernmost township of Johannesburg, to Sandton is fifty-three kilometres.

Leaving early, arriving late: Avhapfani commutes by bus

Avhapfani lives with his family in Protea Glen, a part of Soweto. He works at the Sandton Public Library. Each day he commutes to Sandton by bus. Because he leaves his home early and comes back late, he rarely has time left to spend with his family.

Mode of commute:	bus
Distance to Sandton:	37 kilometres
Travel time:	2.25–3 hours
Average travel speed:	12–17 kilometres/hour
Cost:	R 14

"I started commuting to Sandton seven years ago. Back then, there was not much traffic. But with the World Cup in 2010, things changed a lot. Traffic increased and it has remained since then.
For me, it is difficult because I commute from Soweto to Sandton each day by bus and taxi. While I get from Soweto to Rosebank quickly, the distance from Rosebank to Sandton sometimes takes more than an hour because the bus gets stuck in traffic.
Using the Gautrain is not an option for me. It is too expensive—in fact more than double the price compared to buses and taxis. Sandton is a great place, but the distance from home is my concern. I am not sure if the festival will affect me, because I commute by public transport anyway."

Avhapfani

Avhapfani lives in a newly built house in an extension of Protea Glen. He walks several kilometres from his house to the bus stop. The bus to Sunninghill via Sandton arrives. "I have a monthly ticket, making the bus a cheaper option for me than the taxi."

After a one hour ride through Soweto, the Johannesburg CBD appears on the horizon. The bus circumvents the CBD on the western side and enters into the wealthy suburbs of north Johannesburg. Close to Rosebank, the traffic increases substantially, and the bus gets stuck in a traffic jam.

To avoid further traffic jams, the bus takes a detour through residential neighbourhoods. The branches and leaves of the tree bump against the bus. Many taxis take the same route. However, at the next junction north of Rosebank, the bus needs to enter the clogged main street again.

After getting off the bus in Sandton, he says: "I can never be sure that I arrive on time. My manager understands the issue. But when I am in charge of opening the library in the morning, I have to take a bus earlier, to make sure that I arrive on time."

Commuting costs in South Africa

by Andrew Kerr, DataFirst, University of Cape Town[1]

The fact that a substantial fraction of South African workers live far from their workplaces means that travel to work is costly in terms of time and money. This problem is partly a result of the apartheid and pre-apartheid policies that separated different racial groups—mainly by moving black, coloured, and Indian households away from urban centres. More than twenty years after the end of apartheid, black South Africans still live farther away from jobs than other race groups.

The following discussion[2] uses data from three nationally representative surveys to describe changes in commuting patterns and commuting costs in South Africa between 1993 and 2013.[3]

High commuting times in South Africa

In 2003, black South Africans spent an average of eighty-eight minutes per day commuting to and from work (National Travel Survey [NTS] 2003). This was almost double the average commute time in the US in 2002. On average, in the same year, white South Africans spent fifty-four minutes per day commuting (NTS 2003). Ten years later, average commuting times had increased by a further fourteen minutes for both black and white South Africans (NTS 2013).

How do commuters get to work?

Driving private cars and using minibus taxis were the two most important forms of commuting in 2013. Together, these two forms of transport account for almost 50 per cent of commuting. Walking, whilst important, has hence become a less common way of getting to work—only 20 per cent of commuters

walked to work in 2013 compared to 28 per cent in 1993. In the same time period, the percentage of those commuting by car has increased.

People who use public transport—i.e., those who travel by train and bus—generally spend much longer time commuting than those who drive in cars. Minibus taxi users also spend more time in transit than those in cars, but considerably less than those using the bus or train.

The monetary costs of getting to work

Commuting costs money and time. Commuters who drive cars, use taxis, or multiple modes of transport—usually a combination of bus, train, and taxi—to get to work spend an average of more than 15 per cent of their gross income getting to work (NTS 2013).

The time and monetary costs of transport can be thought of as a kind of "tax" that commuters pay on the incomes that they earn from work. This "tax" varies between modes of transport (and levels of income). High costs of commuting (in terms of time and money) can thus lower the returns to work and may decrease the number of people who are willing to work or look for work.

Does the subsidisation of public transport help?

The implicit "tax" effect of transport costs and time could be reduced by transport subsidies. Public subsidies are distributed to bus and train operators. Minibus taxi operations are not subsidised, although they carried around 71 per cent of all commuters travelling by collective modes of transportation in 2013. They receive only about 1 per cent of the total direct public transport spending by the government in the form of the scrap-and-replacement allowance for old taxis.[4] However, minibus taxis benefit from spending on the road network.

Policies that improve public transport, encourage the densification of cities and towns, better target subsidies for public transport, and allow poor commuters to live closer to work could contribute to reducing the cost and times of commuting.

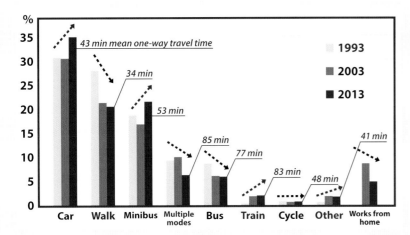

Figure 1: Mean one-way travel time by mode and year

1 Andrew.kerr@uct.ac.za. This is an abridged version of an article that appeared on the online policy forum Econ3x3.org.

2 Andrew Kerr, "Tax(i)ing the poor? Commuting costs in South Africa". REDI paper 12, 2015.

3 1993 Project for Statistics on Living Standards and Development (PSLSD) by The Southern Africa Labour and Development Research Unit (SALDRU) and 2003 and 2013 National Travel Surveys (NTS) by Statistics South Africa

4 South African Department of Transport. 2013. National Road Based Public Transport Transformation Plan: from bus to public transport subsidization. National Council of Provinces presentation, 19 March 2013

A tale of two trains: Phylis commutes by rail

Phylis works at the Sandton Public Library and commutes from Germiston, east of Johannesburg CBD, by Metrorail and Gautrain. Her father takes her to the station from home by car. Earlier, she used to commute by minibus taxi, but after she was involved in an accident, she avoids taxis for long distances. She commutes by a special business train, which costs three times the fare of the common train—but it is clean, safe, and not crowded.

Mode of commute:	train
Distance to Sandton:	25 kilometres
Travel time:	1.5–2 hours
Travel speed:	12–17 km/h
Cost:	R 18 + R 28

There is a long queue at the ticket counter. The ticket allows Phylis to enter a fenced-off platform that is dedicated to higher-class commuter trains. While this platform is almost empty, other platforms are completely crowded. Train announcements do not exist and the displays do not function.

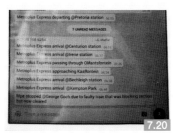

Not long after the train departed, it stops on the open track. "The only way to know what's going on is a WhatsApp group run by other commuters specifically for this train", explains Phylis. This time, a signal failure is the reason for the delay.

The train frequently stops again and halts for long times at intermediate stations. "You can never predict how long it will take to reach Park Station. The stretch is heavily travelled and the system is in bad shape". After more than an hour, the train finally reaches. Phylis hurries through Park Station to get to the Gautrain Station.

At the Gautrain station, Phylis doesn't have to wait long for her train. "The Gautrain is expensive, but I have no other option since Metrorail has stopped running the free bus shuttle for Business Express users from Park Station to Sandton." After an eight-minute ride, she arrives in Sandton.

From the Sandton Gautrain station, she only has to walk a few hundred metres to the library. "Usually I travel via Johannesburg CBD. But when I know that I have to work late in the evening when it is dark, I try to avoid Metrorail because I don't feel safe. I take the car to Rhodesfield and catch the Gautrain there."

Moving together: the festival links people and places

The City of Johannesburg tackles the challenges of socio-spatial divides that run through the metropolitan region by investing in its public and non-motorised transport infrastructure. The EcoMobility World Festival in Sandton was a major element in gaining support for this strategy and boosting its implementation.

In a city where low-income and disadvantaged groups often live far away from income opportunities, affordable transport is essential for the survival of the poorest and the uplift of marginalised communities. Only by securing access to safe, reliable, and efficient transport options can the enormous income inequalities in Johannesburg be reduced in the long run. Mobility is also a matter of dignity. Those who have always walked, cycled, and used public transport for their commutes—often because of having no other choice—should not be neglected and further disadvantaged by poor services and amenities.

In order to provide high-quality and affordable transport services, a bus rapid transit system was implemented in Johannesburg. Since 2009, three trunk routes of the Rea Vaya (meaning "we are going") have been linking Soweto with the Johannesburg inner city, major universities, employment and administrative centres, and popular entertainment facilities. Complementary and feeder bus routes provide convenient connections to other inner-city destinations and other parts of Soweto. Because the trunk routes consist of dedicated lanes for Rea Vaya, the buses are fast and reliable. New routes are being implemented connecting Johannesburg CBD, Alexandra, Sandton, Ivory Park, and Randburg.

The EcoMobility World Festival 2015 actively engaged with the socio-spatial divides of the city. Various events, cycle trainings, learning and entertainment programmes for children, a volunteer programme, and the enhancement of cycling and walking infrastructure were some of the festival components that specifically aimed to highlight social inequalities and empower disadvantaged communities.

△
The Rea Vaya BRT has separate lanes and access points and is a safe, affordable, and fast travel option.

"If you want a city where people live together and work together nicely, you have to change the spatial planning. Our use of cars is historical, we want to rewrite that history. We want people to say, 'they worked towards fostering economic development and encouraging that people are living together'. We are writing that history today. The EcoMobility Festival is one of the first chapters of that history."
Sipho Nhlapo, operations manager for mobility and freight, Johannesburg Roads Agency

"The EcoMobility World Festival is the moment to showcase alternative modes of transport. Social integration and social cohesion are at the centre of that. We need to build our cities and human settlements in a way that they easily promotes people interacting, walking, and cycling."
David Makhura, premier, Gauteng Province, South Africa

Enabling mobility: the Corridors of Freedom

The City of Johannesburg has started retrofitting and "restitching" the city. The "Corridors of Freedom" initiative aims to change the current entrenched settlement patterns and put an end to urban sprawl and uncontrolled spread of low-density developments. In 2013, Mayor Parks Tau announced this programme, which, in his words, "will forever change the urban structure of Johannesburg and eradicate the legacy of apartheid spatial planning". The envisaged results are increased social and cultural interaction and equal access and prosperity irrespective of race and gender. Transport plays a major role in this endeavour. The "Corridors of Freedom" initiative is based on the concept of transit-oriented development: transport corridors connect strategic nodes through accessible, affordable, and time-saving mass transit that includes both bus and passenger rail. Economic growth points, mixed income housing, and public facilities—such as schools, clinics, offices, community facilities, parks, and public spaces—will be set up along the corridors and within the nodes.

The corridors particularly aim at bringing members of marginalised communities closer to job opportunities. In consultation with citizens, the corridors from Johannesburg CBD to Soweto, Alexandra, and the southern Johannesburg mining belt have been identified for urgent intervention. The corridor between Alexandra and Sandton is also among those to be developed in the coming years. In the long term, further corridors will be developed between the township of Diepsloot, Randburg, and Sandton CBD.

Besides upgrading the suburban rail system, the transport strategy of the Corridors of Freedom focuses on bus rapid transit and non-motorised transport. The objectives match with the provisions of the Gauteng Master Transport Plan, which requires every municipality to build at least ten kilometres of non-motorised transport infrastructure each year. In Soweto, five kilometres of cycling lanes have recently been built, linking schools to other public amenities, the Rea Vaya BRT, and rail transport system. Fifteen kilometres of walking and cycling paths are being built in Orange Farm in the far south of Johannesburg.

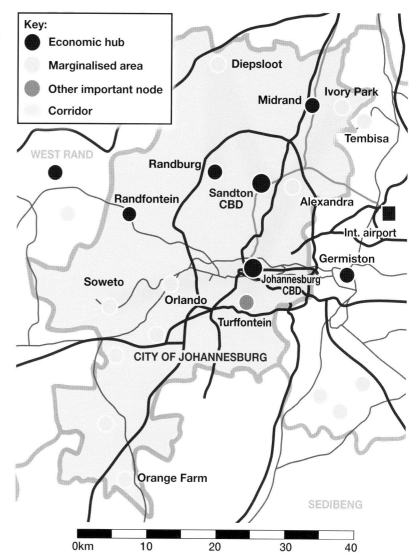

Key:
- ● Economic hub
- ○ Marginalised area
- ◉ Other important node
- Corridor

Alexandra and Sandton: worlds apart, but closely linked

Alexandra—locally known as "Alex"—is a small, but densely populated area in northern Johannesburg, located next to wealthy suburbs and large industrial estates. It is Johannesburg's oldest township and it is just six kilometres from Sandton. Since its foundation in 1912—back then far outside the city—Alexandra has always been among the first destinations for immigrants from other parts of southern Africa, in terms of finding shelter. Moreover, Alexandra's residents have played an important role in the struggle for democracy.

While Sandton is one of the wealthiest places in South Africa, Alexandra is one of the poorest. Many inhabitants of Alexandra find jobs in the offices, hotels, and restaurants of Sandton as low-skilled workers. Public transport between the two places is only provided by informal minibus taxis, which run their fifteen or twenty-two-seater vans every hour of the day. Although relatively cheap, these services are not affordable for all. Thus, around 10,000 people from Alexandra working in Sandton walk and cycle the six-kilometre stretch every day—or night.

The City of Johannesburg seized the EcoMobility World Festival as an opportunity to shed light on this connection between Alexandra and Johannesburg. As part of the "Corridors of Freedom" programme, the City started to build a three-metre-wide dedicated walking and cycling path, equipped with lighting, benches, and hawkers' stalls. For the safety of the users, CCTV cameras will be placed along the route. For the festival, the new path was temporarily extended into the centre of the Sandton CBD, by giving pedestrians and cyclists priority on Maude Street. This was to be made permanent after the festival.

A dedicated cycling and footbridge to cross the motorway is currently under construction. Once this link between Alex and Sandton is completed, commuters from Alexandra will reach their workplaces and homes more comfortably and safely than before. During the construction of the bridge, a tragic incident occurred: the scaffolding of the bridge collapsed during the festival and fell on the busy motorway, causing the death of three people and injuring twenty.

The "Corridor of Freedom" will be further strengthened by the extension of the Rea Vaya rapid bus system from the city centre via Alexandra to Sandton in 2017. Then, a long-needed high-capacity, low-cost public transport option for Alexandra will become reality.

Key Facts Alexandra
Established: 1912
Area: 6.91 square kilometres
Population (2011): 180,000
(unofficial estimates range between 180,000 and 750,000)
99 per cent African

"I personally used to walk from Alexandra township to Sandton in the early nineteen-eighties, crossing Greyston Bridge. It wasn't by choice then and it must be by choice now."

David Makhura, premier, Gauteng Province

▽
Image of the future pedestrian and cycling bridge

Streets Alive: JOZI We-R-1

The Streets Alive Parade was organised on the day of the festival opening to link the two neighbouring districts of Sandton and Alexandra. The parade motivated different people to walk together to Alexandra and make the strong statement that no matter how different the two areas might be, they depend on each other and belong to the same proud city of Johannesburg. The march was also dedicated to the over 10,000 people that walk from Alex to Sandton on a daily basis.

Headed by political leaders of South Africa, Gauteng Province, and the City of Johannesburg, the parade proceeded from West Street in Sandton to the San Kopane Community Centre in the heart of Alexandra. The parade was joined by hundreds of Johannesburgers from all over the city, including many Alexandra residents and international festival visitors who cycled and walked the entire six-kilometre stretch. Dancing groups, marching bands, stilt walkers, and puppeteers turned the parade into a vibrant and carnival-like event full of joy and excitement.

"The festival made people understand how social cohesion can take place"

"While I was walking in the parade, there was one aspect that excited me most. I saw these young people coming on skateboards. They were black and white young people together, their bodies were in motion; it was like poetry. Also there were a lot of white people cycling; together they went right into Alexandra! The festival made people understand how social cohesion can take place and how this division of people based on skin colour can be overcome. A skateboard can bring people together, if the road space is available and if they have the freedom to interact with each other.

In linking Alexandra, a very poor community, to the richest square mile of Africa, the spirit of Nelson Mandela comes alive. As a young man, Mandela lived in Alexandra after coming to Johannesburg from the Eastern Cape. He lived in a small room, which is now a heritage site. Here, he was part of the bus boycott in 1957, when the people of Alexandra said that the bus fares were too high. Later, Mandela said that this was the moment when he turned from being just an observer into a participant in the dialogue."

Christine Walters, MMC for transport, City of Johannesburg

"When you walk, you will never be late"

Xolane Sibanda is one of the young, unemployed people from Alexandra who volunteered as guide at the EcoMobility World Festival. Although transport was arranged for him, he agreed to walk from his home in Alexandra to his workplace at the festival, highlighting the difficulties that 10,000 walking commuters face every day.

"When I was working in Rosebank, I used to take a taxi, but I was always late due to traffic. By taxi it took me forty-five minutes. When I walked, I arrived earlier, because I could just pass the cars that were stuck in the street. When you walk, you save time and you will never be late. However, there was a lot of traffic and the streets are very narrow, so it was very dangerous. The situation on the roads is very bad. People get knocked over by cars in the streets, accidents are prevalent, and people are angry; we see a lot of road rage."

Mode of commute:	walk
Distance to Sandton:	6 kilometres
Travel time:	1 hour 15 minutes
Travel Speed:	5 kilometres/hour
Cost:	R 0

Together with his son, mother, and sisters, Xolane lives in a small house in the middle of Alexandra. Walking through the neighbourhood, he greets almost every person on the street. "I am little bit of a celebrity in my neighbourhood. Everybody knows me", says the charismatic young man.

"I think the festival is a good initiative by the City. Ecomobility will make it safer, healthier, and more convenient for us pedestrians who don't own private cars. Through the festival, measures like widening of the sidewalks are giving us pedestrians back our dignity. When we have many cars in our streets, it is so difficult to be mobile, to move. I don't know what eco means, but mobility means movement, they want us to move freely. Also it reduces air pollution and is good for fitness. It prevents heart problems and other health hazards. It would be good if they introduced ecomobility in the townships also. Alex is very tiny, but many people own cars. They could expand the road for pedestrians, cyclists, and public transport. If ecomobility were introduced in townships, it would change people's mindsets and how they think about the government."

After twenty minutes, he passes by the Pan African Shopping Centre, a bustling commercial area. Leaving Alexandra, Xolane walks through the industrial area of Wynberg, from where Sandton is already visible on the horizon. The sidewalks are newly refurbished and convenient to walk. New street lighting and a cycle track have been set up.

At Greyston Bridge, Xolane crosses the main motorway between Johannesburg and Pretoria. The sidewalk is narrow and in a bad state. Cars leaving the motorway speed by the pedestrians. Next to the big overpass, the new cycle and footbridge is already under construction. After further twenty minutes along wealthy neighbourhoods, Xolane reaches the border of the CBD.

Awareness, learning, and training are the keys to empowerment

A prerequisite for the successful diffusion of ecomobility options is knowledge about existing transport alternatives and how to use them. Those who have never ridden a bus may find it difficult to read a timetable or locate the bus stop. Every cyclist remembers the first painful attempt to ride a bike. Thus, awareness and training are key—both for those who wish to abandon their cars and those who seek to enhance the experience of moving in an ecomobile fashion.

The City of Johannesburg specifically targets young South Africans from disadvantaged communities to be economically empowered. The City builds on the benefits of non-motorised transport to bring them closer to jobs to enable social and economic uplift. Besides providing adequate infrastructure, the City partners with businesses to mobilise funds for donations of bicycles to people in need.

The first Bicycle Empowerment Centre in Orlando, Soweto, was established in 2014 in co-operation with the organisers of the Freedom Ride. This centre provides the necessary training and services to cyclists and creates new economic opportunities.

As part of the EcoMobility Exhibition, vehicle testing and bicycle training were offered, including traffic safety training. During the last week of the festival—when the exhibition moved to Alexandra—2,300 children visited. Assisted by volunteers, many of the children rode a bicycle for the first time in their lives.

Part of the exhibition was the museum "Our History of Transport", a mobile, interactive programme that targeted children and adults alike. On walking tours through Sandton, while playing the "Sandton Scamper" board game, or in storytelling sessions, young and old were exposed to the *culture* of mobility. While learning more about transport in a hands-on and playful manner, people were invited to contemplate the benefits and disadvantages of different forms of transport and one's own mobility behaviour, needs, and preferences.

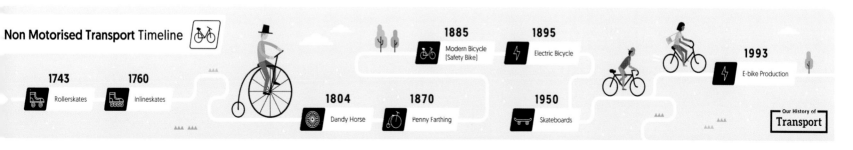

The minibus taxi industry: a response to apartheid planning

Minibus taxis are a form of para-transit that exists in many African countries and are the main mode of collective transport for the black communities of Johannesburg. The characteristic fifteen to twenty-two-seat minibus vans are operated by a variety of entrepreneurs through associations.

The taxi routes are usually fixed, but schedules or route maps do not exist. Commuters can board or alight from the vehicle at any point along the route. Driven by the impetus of making profit, the taxis operate on high-demand routes and go to the inner city, where they get passengers in both directions. Many commuters have to change at least once to reach their destination. Because each trip has to be paid separately, many people spend a considerable share of their income on their daily travel.

The informal or barely publicly regulated minibus taxi sector emerged during the apartheid period. The official public transport services to, from, and within the townships had a poor standard—only offering destinations for commuters and not catering to schools, recreation, shopping, or to new developing areas that required labour. As a response, those who owned vehicles started to transport people in the mid-nineteen-eighties. To control the expanding sector, the government started to distribute licences to the operators and tried to fix the routes. Most of these attempts failed. The sector survived after the end of apartheid, often being the only mode available and a convenient service because people could be picked up and dropped close to their homes or work places.

Today, the minibus taxi industry has an ambivalent position in Johannesburgers' everyday lives. The majority of the white population shuns the taxis and only recognises them when they attract attention due to reckless driving. Many users feel uncomfortable, because the vehicles are often in bad condition and prone to accidents. Violent conflicts between taxi associations over the most lucrative routes have further scared users. However, the sector is an essential element of the region's transport system, and many people still have no other option. The suburban railway is an option to many commuters; however, it is still awaiting comprehensive rehabilitation.

The City of Johannesburg has intensified its efforts to co-operate with the minibus taxi sector. The administration recognises the complex organisational structure of the industry, perceives the taxi associations as partners, and tries to jointly discuss the future of public transport in Johannesburg. The implementation of the Rea Vaya rapid bus system is the result of a collaborative effort by the city government and the taxi associations serving the Soweto region. The associations are co-owners of the company, and the buses are driven by former taxi drivers. The Rea Vaya negotiations have laid the foundation for a new culture of stakeholder collaboration in terms of transport planning in the city.

"Minibus taxis are part of the public transport system, they are an invaluable partner. But with the Gautrain and the BRT systems, people are beginning to experience a different kind of transport system. There will be a major culture shift in the next three to five years. We are going to see a better integration between the minibus taxi industry, the BRT, railway, cycling, and walking."

Ismail Vadi, MEC for roads and transport, Province of Gauteng

◁
Minibus drivers wait in front of the Sandton Transport Interchange until they are called by the dispatcher to enter the station.

Driving people, driving change: the integration of the minibus taxi industry

For the EcoMobility World Festival, the City partnered with the minibus taxi industry. One hundred taxis provided free minibus taxi services in and around Sandton, as well as from the Park & Ride sites. Modern, comfortable, and safe minibus vans were used for the festival services. Besides the taxi drivers, personnel were deployed to assist users at each stop and Park & Ride facility. These station marshals normally work as marshals and dispatchers at taxi ranks all over Johannesburg. After the festival, drivers and marshals returned to their former work locations.

The integration of taxi operators into the festival proceedings was a bold and long-sighted decision. It expresses the spirit of departure from the old mutual animosity between the taxi sector and the city government. For some—particularly the white middle class from the northern suburbs of Johannesburg—it was the first time that they had been exposed to informal transport. Many uttered astonishment about the reliability of the service and the professionalism and kindness of the staff. It is possible that the festival ignited a change of popular attitude towards the minibus sector.

▽ ▷
The minibus taxis were branded with the logo and the colours of the festival for easy identification. The drivers and marshals in festival T-shirts assisted commuters for easy rides.

"Earlier, the taxi industry was marginalised, now the city is partnering with us"

Peter Mabe represents one of the biggest taxi associations in Johannesburg; 1,470 operators are members of the association, owning 2,687 vehicles. Mabe's taxi association operates in the Johannesburg CBD, in parts of Soweto and western Johannesburg, and serves around 480,000 people daily. The association has been involved in developing the first phase of the Rea Vaya BRT system and is a shareholder of the company.

"The most important thing is that the taxi industry accepts and embraces change. The City of Johannesburg is driving that change and we really appreciate it. Earlier, the taxi industry was marginalised and we were never asked when the City rolled out plans. That has changed completely; now the City is partnering with us. That is why we also participate in the EcoMobility Festival.

The executive director for transport approached me, told me about the festival and asked me if we wanted to participate. I said yes. The festival is an opportunity to present our services to motorists and encourage them to start using these services. We need to teach people how to use the minibus taxis, and we need to convince them that we provide quality transport services."

Riding in the spirit of Nelson Mandela: the Freedom Ride

On a Sunday in October, more than 4,000 cyclists braved the hot weather and made their way through the diverse neighbourhoods of Johannesburg. Some of them were clad in professional cycling gear; others were on flower-decorated bicycles or accompanied by their children. They were all part of the Fourth Johannesburg Freedom Ride, which started in the Sandton CBD, passed by the Johannesburg Zoo, Parkview, Forest Town, Hillbrow, Yeoville, and the township of Alexandra before climbing back up the hill of Sandton— twenty-seven kilometres in total.

The Johannesburg Freedom Ride has taken place biannually since February 2014, when the first Freedom Ride to Soweto took place—shortly after the death of Nelson Mandela.

While many cyclists in Johannesburg see cycling as a sport, the Freedom Ride promotes cycling as a mode of urban transport and brings together people of different economic and social classes to celebrate the legacy of Nelson Mandela. The cyclists get to experience Johannesburg's social diversity, by riding along historically important landmarks and disadvantaged neighbourhoods. The initiative was brought to life by cycling activists in partnership with the City of Johannesburg. The event series is sponsored by the City of Johannesburg, and organised in partnership with the insurance company Hollard and Qhubeka, the World Bicycle Relief's programme in South Africa. Funds raised during the Freedom Ride are used to set up Bicycle Empowerment Centres and bicycle distribution programmes in lower income areas.

"We have been supporting the Freedom Ride from its beginning. Our mission is to promote cycling as an alternative for mobility and transport in the city—not just for those who have money, but also for people who do not have other forms of travelling."
Adrian Enthoven, chairman, Hollard Insurance Company Ltd

"The idea of the Freedom Ride is to connect communities. It is a social ride, and it is free for everyone. We want to break the social barriers that were created in South Africa's past. So we ride from the more upper-class communities like Sandton, into areas like Soweto or Alexandra where there is that past, that history, that heritage. We want people to go into these spaces and experience them. That is what connects communities and breaks barriers. "
Muhammed Suleman, Linkd Environmental Services

"We use the Freedom Ride as a way of connecting different communities— rich and poor, black and white, different parts of the city. It is not a race. It is a social ride, it is a relaxed way of just being together on your bikes on the road. The message is that everyone can ride. It is the most democratic form of transport that is available."
Crispian Olver, Cycle Jozi Forum

"If gender is neglected in planning, there will be more cars on the streets"

"In the African perspective, women play a very big role in sustaining and taking care of their families. Accordingly, they have many mobility needs: fetching water, going to the market, taking children to school, and going to the health facility. Women are moving a lot. For every kind of improvement in transport, the specific needs of women need to be considered. If public transport is very bad, inefficient, and rough—the way it is in Africa—you are going to have few women choosing to board the van or the minibus taxi when they are elderly or pregnant. They need to have comfortable public transport, otherwise they will choose to buy a car when they are planning to get pregnant.

When we women are walking on the streets at night, we feel less safe compared to men. Because of this women tend to avoid walking, which means they are already excluded from some form of mobility. Keeping in mind that they are moving with a purpose, this exclusion means that their development is being sabotaged in one way or the other.

Some societies in Africa believe that women should not ride a bicycle. If they don't ride cycles as girls, they won't do as women either. It also means that their children will not ride. So if you are implementing cycle lanes, there is a group of people who are not going to use them.

When policies for ecomobility come into place and we start preparing plans, the gender aspect has to be given a central role. Otherwise women will use cars."

Amanda Ngabirano Aziidah, Makerere University, Kampala, Uganda

Dropped off at the doorstep: Xolani's daily commute by minibus taxi

Xolani works in a hotel in Sandton and lives in Alexandra. Each day in the early morning, she commutes to Sandton by minibus taxi. While the taxi trip is short, she has to walk twenty minutes from her house to the minibus station. The ride costs between R 8 to 10 one way, depending on the size of the vehicle. Reduced fares for commuters are not common in the informal transport sector. For a low-income worker like her, R 20 daily travel expenses are a considerable part of her monthly budget. However, she prefers the taxi to walking, because she also needs time to take care of her family.

The minibus taxi station ("taxi rank") is located on the roof of Alexandra's largest shopping centre. There are no signs to indicate the taxis to Sandton, but Xolani knows where they park. One 16-seater van has just filled, so she has to wait for the next one, which is already approaching. As the ride begins, passengers pass the fare to the driver's assistant.

Mode of commute:	minibus taxi
Distance to Sandton:	8 kilometres
Travel time:	45 minutes
Travel speed:	11 kilometres/hour
Cost:	R 9

While the change money is distributed among the occupants, the first passengers prepare to get off as the taxi approaches Sandton. There are no dedicated stops along the route, but the taxi halts frequently on demand. The remaining passengers, including Xolani, leave the taxi in the centre of Sandton CBD. From here it is only a few metres to her workplace.

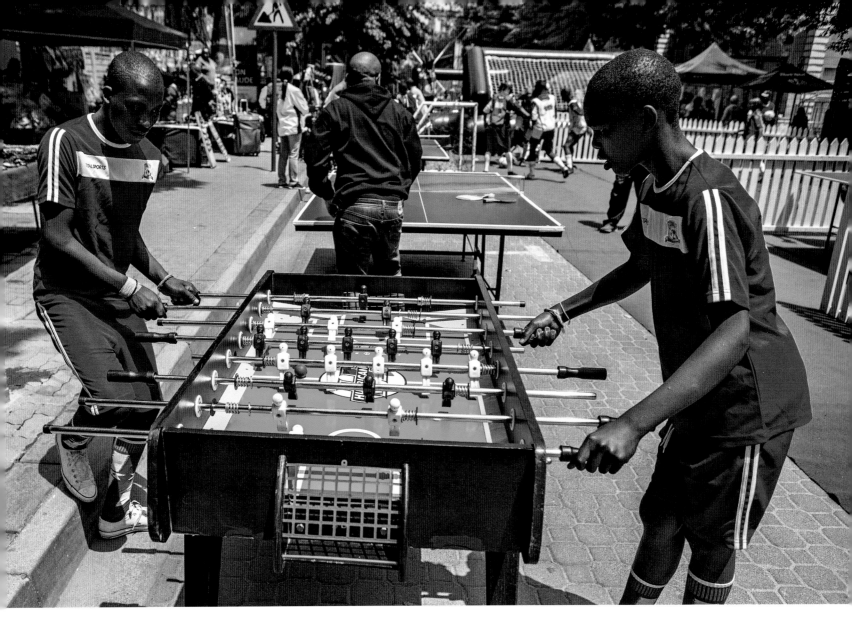

4 **Reclaiming the streets**

"You don't want cities to all look the same; you want them to have their own character and be meaningful to people. We need to create places where you feel safe and comfortable, where people are around you and many things are going on! At the same time, spaces need to be clean, beautiful, and well designed. It is not about having star architecture and fancy buildings; far more important is the space in between the buildings and how to design it. People will begin to use the space and realise that this is actually what the value of living in the city is. They will demand that developers realise the economic benefits of it."

Camilla Ween, urban design and transportation, director, Goldstein Ween Architects, London, UK

▷
Skateboarders enjoy empty Alice Lane in Sandton CBD.

▷
In the final week of the festival, the dreary parking lot of the Sankopano Community Centre in Alexandra was transformed into a lively and colourful exhibition and entertainment area, visited by 2,300 children.

▷
Many South Africans rarely walk and spend time in public space. A mother and her daughter enjoy the safe environment on West Street.

▷▷
Lunch break at a temporary food stall on West Street

Urban public space: for cars or for people?

Public spaces in our cities are dominated by cars. Since the car had its breakthrough as a means of transport for the masses in the second half of the twentieth century, cities in industrialised countries were reshaped to accommodate the car. In most of the growing cities of developing countries, the first reaction to increasing mobility needs is the construction of infrastructure for fast automobility, although it caters only to a small portion of the population.

Vibrant public spaces as well as parklands have been turned into parking lots and multi-lane motorways. They have ceased to deserve the designation "public", because each occupation of space by moving or parked cars is essentially a temporary privatisation of that space that does not allow different activities to take place simultaneously. Advanced auto-dependent societies consist of enclosed islands—shopping malls, office towers, residential enclaves—linked by high-speed motorways. The in-between space is almost an inanimate "non-space", burdened by high noise and pollution levels.

Planners and decision-makers soon realised that automobile-oriented urban development had contributed to the decay of inner cities and reduced the quality of city life. Consequently, strategies for urban revitalisation starting in the nineteen-eighties have dealt with the question of how to reduce the dominance of cars in urban life. Accordingly, the creation of new spaces for interaction and enjoyment is often accompanied by the designation of pedestrian areas and traffic-reduction measures.

Activities related to mobility and non-mobility can easily get along in the same space. This is demonstrated in shared spaces where non-motorised and small motorised movement is prioritised. For example, walking, cycling, and using Segways do not occupy much space and the speed is usually lower compared to cars. Thus, a pedestrian is not disturbing the juggler or the street vendor; rather, they delight each other. Not being enclosed in a car or in a building, actors in the same open space can maintain a sense of mutual respect and responsibility, as well as the ability to recognise and valorise the diversity of the city and its people.

△
The narrow alleys of a traditional market area in Hyderabad are best travelled by ecomobile modes.

◁
Vast parking lot in Bangkok

The loss and rediscovery of Johannesburg's public space

With the end of apartheid, open public spaces have deteriorated in the Johannesburg CBD and the surrounding neighbourhoods. Affluent middle classes had gradually moved further north, and in parts of the inner city—such as Yeoville, Hillbrow, and Berea—poor migrants from other African countries settled in. In the nineteen-nineties, the Johannesburg centre was crime ridden, which had the effect that people began to avoid the inner city, especially in the evening hours.

The deteriorating safety and quality of outside public spaces have supported car-oriented development in Johannesburg. The establishment of a large shopping centre in the open field of Sandton was followed by further shopping malls all over Johannesburg, including Soweto. Easily accessible by car, these indoor spaces have become the new zones of interaction, under the watchful eyes of security guards. Auto dependency also fostered the establishment of low-density and mono-functional residential areas, where there is no activity in the street except for domestic workers walking to the bus stops.

Yet Johannesburg is now revalorising its open spaces. Citizens' groups, artists, and community workers are among those who reclaim city spaces for temporary activities. In Jeppestown, a poor neighbourhood east of the Johannesburg CBD, artists have painted the walls of old warehouses and thereby beautified the urban environment. Melville, Rosebank, and Maboneng bustle with street cafés and a vibrant nightlife. Once again, Johannesburgers can enjoy the warm and dry climate in open spaces.

▷
Wall mural in Jeppestown

◁▽
The snack stall in Sandton's Maude Street is a popular meeting point for office workers.

▽
The Maboneng Precinct attracts visitors with street cafés and restaurants.

Reclaiming the streets with music, fun, and company: festival events

Having fewer cars on the roads returns the space to people and to ecomobile ways of moving. The EcoMobility Festival offered an idea of what Johannesburg would look like if people-friendly policies were implemented and citizens reclaimed the streets for uses other than mobility.

Few things are as boring as empty streets. Reclaiming the streets is a learning process, sometimes a challenge, and often a lot of fun. During the festival month, several public events were organised in the closed-off streets of Sandton, mainly on the car-free West Street. Around 15,000 citizens from various parts of Johannesburg appropriated Sandton's streets through these events, which were created together with a wide range of partners.

"We proved that the streets of Johannesburg truly belong to all our citizens and that with innovation and imagination, we can turn streets into amenable public spaces."

Mpho Parks Tau, executive mayor, City of Johannesburg

◁
The festival was officially inaugurated in a grand ceremony on West Street. Music, dance groups, and a poet entertained the spectators.

◁▽
Instead of pavement and cars, West Street hosted basketball courts, table tennis, and a 300-metre-long water slide, which were enjoyed by thousands of citizens of all ages during the Streets Sport Weekend.

▽
The closure of the festival month was celebrated with concerts and a public sports viewing in a giant block party on West Street, which was preceded by a street carnival with an ecomobile theme.

Appropriating street space: temporarily and permanently

Matthew Passmore invented PARK(ing) Day, an annual event where citizens, artists, and activists temporarily transform parking spaces into public parklets. Konrad Otto-Zimmermann, the creative director of the EcoMobility Festivals, discussed with him ways of reclaiming and rededicating street space to uses beyond mobility—temporarily or permanently.

KOZ You invented PARK(ing) Day. How did you come up with this idea?

MP I was working in a high-rise building in downtown San Francisco from which I could see cars and delivery trucks coming and going down in the street. I thought: what if instead of vehicles, a park or an art gallery would be there for a few minutes? What if the streets were used in a different way than for storing vehicles? It seemed obvious, we had to build a park within this area! It is a way to take action to help our city to create more green space—even if just temporarily.

KOZ How did you transform the space, was it a long process of co-ordinating with the city?

MP It was a secret. The park suddenly popped up. We legally rented the metred parking space and only stayed for the length of the lease. After those two hours, we packed up and left. The action went viral in the Internet. Two months later, the City told us: "We love the idea and give you our support. But keep it as a guerrilla art project. Otherwise, the rules and regulations will strip away the spirit of the idea."

KOZ The project idea quickly spread around the world.

MP Lots of people contacted us to do similar projects. In 2006 we said, let's organise all of this interest on a single day and make a global statement on the use of urban space. We realised that car congestion, the use of urban space, and the amount of urban space allotted to automobile infrastructure are issues that are faced by many cities around the world.

KOZ PARK(ing) Day certainly inspired the idea of the EcoMobility World Festivals. Another source of inspiration was a project by the Munich-based architect Hermann Grub. He occupied all of the parking spaces in the iconic Kurfürstendamm Boulevard in west Berlin with rented cars. Overnight, he covered all those cars with roll-out grass. People went to their offices the next morning and found a different cityscape! That picture of temporarily changing urban space led me to the idea of having real people in a real city playing their real life, just with the changed condition of ecomobility.

MP I love that the festival idea was inspired by a piece of art. It is a living prototype of what ecomobility could be. It is not just like reading a book to people or telling them a story—they are fully engrossed in this possibility; they are living it!

△
Konrad Otto-Zimmermann (right) discusses temporary and permanent street transformations with Matthew Passmore (left).

KOZ When the first EcoMobility World Festival in Suwon ended in September 2013, some people were in tears and said it should go on forever. The mayor did something interesting. He thanked the residents and said, "I requested you do this for a month. You fulfilled my wish and it was a great success. Now we turn it around. You tell us how you want your neighbourhood to look and the City will implement it." A large roundtable session showed that the residents wanted speed limits and parking restrictions. The City put plant containers along the sidewalks so that no car can misuse the sidewalks and the space for pedestrians is kept safe. Because driving and parking became less convenient, many people now walk instead and fill the streets with life!

MP It will be interesting to see how the City and the citizens in Johannesburg continue after the festival.

KOZ The area that Mayor Parks Tau chose for Johannesburg is quite the opposite of the Suwon case. Nonetheless, I experienced something similar. What I proposed as a transport-oriented project turned out to be a social project, a collective learning project, and an institutional learning project. The discussions around it have become part of the real value of the festival, and they remain. Now the City and the citizens can move forward with deciding how to use public space.

5 Building partnerships for urban improvement

"We not only changed the way we move, but also the way we do things as a city."

Lisa Seftel, executive director for transport, City of Johannesburg

▷
Lisa Seftel (City of Johannesburg) with stakeholders during a planning meeting in the festival area

▷
During the *Mayor's Imbizo*, Johannesburg's citizens could raise concerns, ask questions, and report experiences concerning the EcoMobility World Festival.

▷
A group of people with disabilities test the improved facilities on West Street.

▷▷
Carol Snyman and Maletlabo Handel (SANEDI), Alex Bhiman (City of Johannesburg), Santhosh Kodukula and Steven Brand (ICLEI) collaborated for the EcoMobility Exhibition.

Participation for inclusive urban development

The path to sustainable urban development is long and often bumpy. It requires long-term decision-making that touches many social, ecological, and economic aspects of the city. Different and sometimes diverging priorities, interests, and viewpoints need to be balanced. As a form of urban governance, participatory planning, and stakeholder involvement processes are often initiated by local governments to inform the public and raise support for public projects. But participation and involvement can go far beyond that: they open up opportunities to work jointly on a topic or project and to create collaborative partnerships between authorities, businesses, and citizens.

To be successful, such an iterative process requires the involvement of a maximum number of urban stakeholders and actors. This includes not only departments of the local and regional governments, the business community, non-governmental organisations, and citizens' initiatives, but also ordinary citizens who are not a part of any organisation. Urban development processes can affect some population groups more—especially if they are already marginalised, have special needs, or have fewer possibilities to raise their voices publicly. Bringing women, children, minority groups, people with disabilities, and those who are economically disadvantaged into the discussion is crucial to planning processes.

Transport planning and infrastructure development are often at the centre of controversial discussions within the urban community. Being involved can be a challenging, but highly motivating experience for citizens and other actors. For public authorities, it is often a new field of action and requires opening up highly specialised and complex subject areas for public debate. The role of the urban and transport planner has shifted from primarily drawing the plans to the facilitation of involvement processes.

When successful, participatory planning and stakeholder involvement creates trust in local governments and between different urban actors, empowers communities and leads to better project outcomes that are more responsive to the diverse needs. When all segments of urban society are able to join the debate, participatory planning has the potential to create a joint vision for the city that the majority of the urban society identifies with. This vision can provide a strong guidance for leaders and citizens on the way to a sustainable urban future. Urban planning is then not just regulating the urban environment, but becomes a tool for local democracy and inclusive governance. It unites diverse urban actors into a community that supports a common cause.

In South Africa, the people's right to participate is embedded into the Constitution of 1996. The City of Johannesburg and Gauteng Provincial Legislature have introduced a culture of participation and stakeholder involvement in administrative processes. The strong commitment is expressed in the fact that since 2011 Gauteng has implemented a Children's Parliament, a Women's Parliament, and the Parliament for Persons with Disabilities. The City of Johannesburg has established a central Petitions and Participation Committee and Ward Committees in all of its 130 wards. For transport projects like the Rea Vaya, the public is extensively informed and involved in the planning process. For efficient real-time communication with citizens, the City uses social media widely. Twitter, in particular, allows both citizens and the City to comment and respond on any issue at any place in time, which is especially relevant in emergency situations.

Joining hands for ecomobility

From the beginning, it was clear that a project of this scale could only succeed if stakeholders and partners were brought into the picture as early as possible and were met at eye level.

Stakeholders involved not only came from the field of transport, but from a broad range of backgrounds and topics. Provisions were made for residents' comfort, business operations, street events, communication and media relations, community building, and the involvement of citizens and NGOs. Partnerships were built with the private sector, residential groups, the taxi industry, and different city government departments. The provincial government and agencies were closely involved and supported the programme.

The City integrated the activities of local cycling groups, traffic safety organisations, urban development authorities, universities, and companies in the month-long festival of sporting events, vehicle exhibitions, and test tracks, bike rides, education programmes, concerts, and a family day.

A Political Steering Committee was established, which had political oversight over the process and determined the festival programme's key pillars. By the end of 2014, a Technical Steering Committee was set up to handle the operations. Initially, it met every two weeks, then weekly, then daily, and during the festival even sometimes twice a day. This was important to co-ordinate between the hundreds of people who were engaged in the preparation and execution of the festival project: more than hundred people were involved at the co-ordinating level. About 250 festival guides worked on the grounds, and 90 Johannesburg Police Department officers secured the roads and helped with traffic diversion. Additionally, a lot of people worked behind the scenes, such as caterers, sound engineers, or photographers.

The City's continuous efforts to build partnerships helped to gain the trust of stakeholders and enabled the mutual learning processes that will last long after the festival.

△
Briefing of Johannesburg Metropolitan Police Department officers on the Transport Management Plan before the festival

▽
Final meeting of festival co-organisers before the start of the festival

"It has been amazing to work with very dedicated, energetic, and passionate people."

Lisa Seftel is the executive director of transport for the City of Johannesburg. In this function, she guides the City's transport planning and operational planning and oversees the integration of different transport operators and the Johannesburg Roads Agency. Before and during the festival, Lisa Seftel was the main coordinator. She moderated Steering Committee meetings and was out in the streets to solve conflicts herself. It is impossible to imagine the EcoMobility World Festival without her.

"I am a passionate South African. What I love is that people organise and are active participants in shaping their future. I am very passionate about government getting feedback and interacting with people. And I am very passionate about change.

Some projects need detailed planning, detailed cost-benefit analysis, and risk analysis so that they work and that you don't create white elephants. But you need to mix those projects with what is being called tactical urbanism where you can have short-term interventions. These still have a level of detail and care but can be implemented in a short time and can focus on behavioural change. The Freedom Ride, for example was quickly organised by a group of city officials as well as NGOs and people who are passionate about cycling. The Freedom Ride involves people and changes behaviour; moreover, it shows that we can bring people from different walks of life together in the common interest of cycling and healthy lifestyles.

One of the festival's big legacies for the City of Johannesburg is that people have learnt a lot about how to implement and take a project from an idea to something that is workable and also innovative. It has been amazing to work with very dedicated, energetic, and passionate people."

LOCAL ADMINISTRATION CITY OF JOHANNESBURG

Johannesburg Roads Agency
Johannesburg Metropolitan Police Department
Region E   Johannesburg Development Agency

Community Development   Transport
Emergency Management Services   City Parks
Joburg Property Company   Group Communications

GOVERNMENT

SANEDI   NDOT
Sandton SAPS
Gauteng Dept of Roads
and Transport

EXHIBITION

SANEDI
The Coloured Cube
Pure Grit
over 30 exhibitors

VOLUNTEERS

TRANSPORT

Metrobus   Gautrain   PUTCO
SANTACO Greater
Joburg Region
Top Six Management
MPA   ARUP   Qhubeka
Bophelong   Lenash

SANDTON BUSINESSES & PROPERTY OWNERS

CORE PARTNERS & CONTRACTORS

ICLEI   The Urban Idea
SADMON
Sandton
Management District

DIALOGUES

ICLEI   Hollard
GEF   IDC

EVENTS

Road Safety organisations
South African Police Service
Freedom Ride   Discovery
Hollard   SAB

MONITORING

IBM   Arup
Newsclip   GCRO
Growth Point

RESIDENTS' ASSOCIATIONS

CITIZEN GROUPS

Explaining, listening, collaborating: the stakeholder processes

In order to include the perspectives of all of the groups that have been touched by the festival in and around Sandton, an unprecedented level of citizen and stakeholder involvement was initiated, which called for active participation at various stages. Different formats were chosen to include all voices and to negotiate all needs.

Overall, more than eighty consultations with groups of residents, property owners, businesses, public transport operators, and other stakeholders were held to spread the concept and identify trade-offs with the private sector. Residents and the interested public could raise concerns in public consultation meetings. One of them was the executive mayor's breakfast meeting in March 2015, which was attended by 125 people. During the festival, citizens were asked to participate in the *Mayor's Imbizo*, a moderated public meeting that was broadcasted live. Citizens could ask questions via Twitter or directly in the conference hall, which were answered by the Johannesburg Mayor and a group of international experts.

All forty-five property owners along the affected streets were contacted by the transport department and the Johannesburg Development Agency to inform about the festival plans and to collect information. Moreover, the aim was to understand concerns about the streets to be closed in October 2015, the public transport loop, and the legacy projects. A meeting was also held with informal traders in Sandton. In addition, MMC Christine Walters personally met various executives of large companies and discussed their operational needs: "The initial conversation and dialogues were very hostile in some areas, very difficult, but once we started talking to people, you saw a different frame of mind. Most of them finally bought into the idea. Now we have a plan for the future. Everybody knows the intention, they have given input into the master plan, so it is also theirs and they own it."

"You cannot close the economic hub of Africa": frequently raised concerns

Throughout the stakeholder processes and public consultations, several concerns were raised by commuters, company heads, property owners, transport operators, and nearby residents.

- Will the festival lead to a shutdown of the economic hub of Africa?
- How will the restricted transport options affect commuters' lives?
- How can the businesses trust that their thousands of employees and visitors will be able reach their offices?
- Will property owners face a parking revenue loss in case the City closes some roads to cars?
- Will the altered accessibility lead to financial losses for hotels, malls, and retailers?
- Will residents be able to access their homes?
- Will parents be able to drop their kids off at school?
- How will service delivery contractors access their clients and meet the service level agreements?

More than fifty one-on-one meetings took place, and several traffic arrangements were altered in order to find the best solution for all. The stakeholder process turned out to be one of the long-lasting legacies of the festival—with new partnerships emerging, mutual exchange of experiences and knowledge, as well as an increase in mutual trust.

▷
Lisa Seftel discusses the exhibition with festival partners Chiara M' Crystal and Guido Ceruti from Pure Grit and Spero Patricios from SADMON.

"The festival is great to kick-start what we needed to do anyway"

Elaine Jack is the urban manager for the Sandton Central City Improvement District, which is a private entity that is run by the private property owners within the Sandton CBD. In this function, she is active in the collaboration and consultation processes between the private sector and the City of Johannesburg—for example, when it comes to public space or public amenities in Sandton. For the festival, Jack represented the companies that were affected by changes in the transport management.

"The discussions prior to the festival were very intense. The property owners were concerned about the daily running of business. In the consultations, it was clear that for the property owners to be confident about the change in transport that the City of Johannesburg envisaged, their operational and infrastructural needs had to be secured. In this regard, one key aspect is successful communication. When property owners are informed well in advance, they can plan better and then they can brief those affected—from the tenants to the security guard who comes to work on a daily basis.

Corporations are not really too worried about change, because change happens. I have experienced that the CEOs are a lot more excited about the introduction of changes than the employees. During the stakeholder process, they realised that the project is necessary in the long run for Sandton to remain accessible and competitive. CEOs see a strategic advantage, because their staff members are more productive when they can come by public transport, instead of being frustrated by sitting in a traffic jam. Thus, the festival is a great project to kick-start what we needed to do anyway in the future."

"Good public transport can bring people to work less stressed"

"We have people who commute from Pretoria or East Rand by car. It takes a lot of time to get here and is highly unreliable. People miss meetings or they come too early for meetings. People talk about congestion and frustration and how long you sit in a car to come home. Good public transport can bring people to work less stressed—and this brings huge benefits to the companies.

As a property developer in Sandton, we have been quite involved in the cycle route between Rosebank and Sandton, which is the golden mile in terms of offices and accommodation. The cycle route comes through the back of our building. We are proposing a bridge over Sandton Drive because it is quite a hostile road to get across. The bridge will have a staircase down to the proposed BRT station. If there are linkages between all modes of public transport, they will be much more effective.

Also, we are looking at electric bikes and a charging area outside the Gautrain Station, and we will bring a charging point in front of our building. Growthpoint is also involved with the green building council. They award points for showers in basements and for promoting people coming to work on bikes and other eco-friendly modes of transport. We would love to do a map of Sandton to indicate where these facilities are available, so people in those buildings know that the facilities exist.

What we want as landowners is that ecomobility does not just stop after October, but that the public transport and Park & Ride facilities remain. Ecomobility should provide a part of the long-term solution rather than just being a festival for a short period of time."

Paul Kollenberg, acting director office sector, Growthpoint Properties

"There is a need to work together"

"Most CEOs are thinking quite short term—they think it is a pain to have the roads closed during the festival month. But I am hoping that the festival will cause people to pause, think, and reflect. It is in the interest of businesses to come up with much more efficient ways to move people around in the city in order to enable their businesses to survive—both the businesses that are selling goods and services in the city, as well as businesses that just need their employees to get to the office in the morning.

Our company is located in Parktown and has not been impacted by the festival, unfortunately. But for our employees, we are looking at priority parking for people who do car sharing and carpooling. Also, a lot of people get to our office through other public transport, such as bus or rail. Connecting that last mile either through bike-sharing systems or cycle lanes is also something we are investigating.

While it is often difficult for the City to prioritise ecomobility as a budget item over other essential needs—like housing, water, and energy—the private sector can mobilise significant resources. There is a need to work together, which will be a lot more powerful than everyone just trying to do something on their own."

Adrian Enthoven, chairman, Hollard Insurance Company Ltd

"We have the ability to encourage people to change behaviour"

"As an insurance company, our core purpose about making people healthier is very consistent with physical activity, which is a fantastic by-product of the festival. There is no trade-off with ecomobility: it is good for the environment, it is good for the body, it is good for the country. Hence, we are very supportive of the festival, and I hope that people experience what it is all about. We are trying our best to get people out of their vehicles and on to public transport by using incentives, social capabilities, and active rewards. Our policyholders also get a discount if they drive less and use the Gautrain. Our client base is millions of people; hence, we have the ability to encourage people to change behaviour."

Adrian Gore, chief executive officer, Discovery Ltd

▷ Sandton employees walk from the Gautrain station to their workplaces along West Street. By commuting in an ecomobile fashion, employees arrive at work more relaxed.

"They really wanted it to work": a caring and responsive City

Prior to the festival, as well as during the month-long event, the organisers reacted to concerns, problems, unexpected incidences, and the actual traffic behaviour of commuters, residents, and passers-by, with a participatory and responsive management approach.

This included measures to motivate citizens, alter traffic flow, improvise transport operations, and conduct public debates via social and traditional media. The Organising Committee regularly reviewed the progress and decided on responses, adjustments, and outreach strategies as necessary. Observed reactions (on the roads, in the media, of the citizens) were translated in an interactive, responsive operation in real time. Changes were communicated through mainstream media channels, as well as social media like Twitter.

> "A local ward councillor was concerned that people might protest against the festival. I told him our constitution allows people to raise their opinion and if they want to march, we will accommodate that and I think so far it is going very well."
>
> Christine Walters, MMC for transport, City of Johannesburg

Gautrain
@TheGautrain

⚙ 👤 Follow

Following the collapse onto the M1, The Gautrain Management Agency has decided to operate our bus service free of charge for tomorrow only.

RETWEETS 110   LIKES 36

Amit Chiba
@amitchiba

⚙ 👤 Follow

In response to the #M1BridgeCollapse, I am seriously impressed with @CityofJoburgZA in dealing with this. Free busses, etc. Big thumbs up.

RETWEETS 6   LIKES 10

△
A high degree of responsiveness and emergency management was shown when the scaffolding for the construction of a cycle and foot bridge collapsed on to M1 motorway, not far from Sandton CBD. The construction work was not part of the EcoMobility Festival, however, the bridge is one of the Legacy Projects linking Alexandra and Sandton CBD.
The quick response and flexibility of the city government and the provision of free public transport services to avoid a traffic collapse due to the closed motorway was discussed and complimented in social media.

"If you want something to work, you have to work with the community"

"I live in a residential area just outside the CBD. When the City proposed a Park & Ride area in our community, residents were concerned about security issues, littering, and the breeding area for birds that nest in the ground.

The Ward Councillor and the organisers heard of our concerns and invited us to talk. The committee from the transport department explained to me in detail how they were organising this project, which gave me a better understanding. The meeting was great; we came to a mutual agreement. They kindly offered twelve security guards, agreed to install extra bins and promised to make sure the birds are safe.

The organisers were very co-operative and reasonable. They really wanted it to work. If you want something to work, you have to work with the community and the residents around the area—the City was very good at that. Those who did not want to be involved unfortunately missed out. People need to co-operate with the City. Because when there is no co-operation, the City is on their own to try and make decisions."

Lori Klein, administrator of the Lower Sandhurst Community Association

Making the festival work on the ground: the festival volunteers

The festival would not have been as successful without the support by 250 volunteer festival guides who were present at every venue of the festival, handling most of the day-to-day activities on the ground. They guided visitors through the streets of Sandton, took care of international experts during the EcoMobility Dialogues, assisted in bicycle training sessions, and educated children in the exhibition area.

All festival guides were unemployed youth from the neighbouring Alexandra township and took part in the Vulindlel' eJozi programme, a City of Johannesburg initiative aimed at breaking down barriers to opportunities by providing skill training programmes and entry-level employment. Prior to the festival, the volunteers were trained in communication, presentation, and teamwork skills. Some of them developed in ways they had previously not imagined. After the festival, they received certificates and confirmations of employment that will support their entry into the professional workforce. By constantly being in touch with visitors and exhibitors, a few volunteers were offered job opportunities for after the festival.

"Because I spoke with confidence, I found for the first time that people really listened to what I had to say. It was incredible."
Nomusa, worked as an exhibition guide

"We are proud to have contributed to the development of sixteen young South Africans. Their energy and enthusiasm was critical to the success of the exhibitions in Sandton and Alexandra."
Mariapaola McGurk, managing director, The Coloured Cube and curator of "Our History of Transport"

"I became a festival volunteer because I wanted to work and not just sit in the township. Some people I went to school with take drugs or do crime. I did not want to end up in jail or dead. I want to make a good future for my six-year-old son. I want him to be proud of his daddy. Maybe I can open a coffee shop and employ other youth based on my previous jobs and new skills."
Xolane Sibanda, worked at the Dialogues and the Exhibition

6 Global cities act on climate change

"Whether the First or the Third World, we all have to begin to look after our planet, to look after the environment. Transport is the major contributor to carbon emissions. In Gauteng alone, we are contributing up to 4 per cent of carbon emissions on the African continent, just this province. This is not sustainable over the long term. We want to show the world that ecomobility is possible on the African continent. African cities can change."

Ismail Vadi, MEC for roads and transport, Province of Gauteng

▷
During the EcoMobility Dialogues, transport experts discussed innovative urban mobility solutions.

▷
Mayor Parks Tau of Johannesburg and MEC Ismail Vadi during the Mayor's Roundtable

▷
International visitors at the exhibition site

▷▷
Councillor Christine Walters with Deputy Mayor Hong-Mo Wu and Ching-Fu Chen, director general of transport, City of Kaohsiung, Taiwan, in a Rea Vaya bus during the transport tour to Soweto

Urban transport emissions: a contributor to climate change

In many areas of the world, climate change has negative implications—such as droughts, extreme weather events, rise in temperature, and the spread of vector-borne diseases—often hitting those who are already disadvantaged. Governments, city leaders, NGOs, and communities across the globe are trying to find ways both to reduce emissions and adapt to climate change effects. One of the main sources of greenhouse gas emissions is the transport sector, which is responsible for almost 30 per cent of the global energy consumption. According to the latest report by the Intergovernmental Panel on Climate Change (IPCC), transport emissions could increase at a faster rate than emissions from the other energy end-use sectors. A closer look at the data shows that urban transport constitutes roughly 40 per cent of total transport energy consumption. In South Africa, the numbers are even higher: transport in cities accounts for 56 per cent of the country's energy consumption and 16 per cent of the total CO_2 emissions.

Current urban transport is often inefficient and resource intensive, especially in cities where the transport infrastructure is oriented towards private vehicles. The introduction and promotion of ecomobility and more efficient ways of moving through awareness campaigns, infrastructure provision, and urban mobility policies is a major step to decrease urban transport emissions. Local transport initiatives will play an essential role in meeting national transport targets and thus contribute to a global cause.

The City of Johannesburg is well aware of its contributions to greenhouse gas emissions and is strategically looking for options to reduce the city's carbon footprint. Together with other global cities, Johannesburg actively tests and offers solutions not only to local but also global problems. Like his predecessor Amos Masondo, who served as ICLEI's global president for a term, Parks Tau is an active member of ICLEI – Local Governments for Sustainability, the world's leading network of over 1,000 cities, towns, and metropolises committed to building a sustainable future. Johannesburg is an early participant in ICLEI's Cities for Climate Protection Campaign. Parks Tau is also a member in the C40 Climate Change Network Steering Committee and co-president of the Metropolis network, which work towards the reduction of climate change impacts and sustainable and resilient cities respectively.

◁
Emission testing for private vehicles was offered at a Park & Ride site.

"Johannesburg stakeholders are passionate about how they can reduce emissions from traffic"

Santhosh Kodukula (SK) is the manager of the EcoMobility Program for ICLEI – Local Governments for Sustainability. He was the strategic director for the EcoMobility Dialogues programme.

You are working with cities around the globe. What made it special to co-operate with Johannesburg?

SK Working with the City of Johannesburg officials, the professional conference organisers, and the stakeholders was a very enthusiastic and interesting experience. We saw that the Johannesburg stakeholders are very passionate about how they can contribute to the EcoMobility Festival, as well as international discussions on reducing emissions from traffic.

How did the EcoMobility Dialogues contribute to discussions and improvements on a local and global level?

SK Johannesburg wanted to do something different as a conference and came up with the Dialogues, where one theme is discussed in-depth for a whole day. The general public could take part in the sessions and broaden their knowledge. Experts and entrepreneurs from Johannesburg could discuss with international experts how things could be implemented on the ground.
For the Dialogues topics, we kept in mind the different levels of problems and actions—South Africa on a larger scale, Johannesburg as an urban region, and Sandton as a CBD. The Dialogues have done a very good job of answering the local stakeholders about why intervening in a CBD is meaningful for the economic and environmental future of Johannesburg, as well as for the global climate cause.

Which message will you spread among your other member cities?

SK Initially, many people don't know that they have alternatives to cars. When you introduce these options and people start using new forms of mobility, you see their enthusiasm. We will tell our member cities that in order to promote ecomobility, they need to involve stakeholders, plan for alternative transport systems, and make bicycle lanes and footpaths safe so that people have good experiences.

"We want to show the world our personality and that we can commit ourselves"

"Apartheid isolated us from the international community. In the struggle, we had four pillars of liberation. One of the pillars was the support from the international community. Many people from all over the world helped us. We would not have been able to do this without their support, and we appreciate what has been done for us. As a community, we had to come back and say thank you to the world.
Now we want the world to recognise us for who we are. Give us a right to stand firmly as Africa, it is our time now. We want to show the world our personality and that we can commit ourselves. As Africa, as South Africa, and as the city of Johannesburg, we want our voice to be heard.
We have achieved political freedom, but we don't yet have economic and social freedom. We want to be prosperous; therefore we need to empower people economically. We still have to fight for our democracy, because it is very young and it gets tested all the time. So the only way that it can mature is for us to be part of the global village. By 2050 over 80 per cent of our people will be living in urban areas, and we have to learn what other cities are doing in managing this.
Digitalisation and technology are bringing us closer to each other, and we cannot afford to do anything alone anymore. Therefore, the EcoMobility Festival is a key opportunity to bring people together and discuss the issues."

Christine Walters, MMC for transport, City of Johannesburg

International exchange to mitigate climate change

City administrations worldwide discuss how to best achieve common goals of climate change mitigation and adaptation. The festival brought these global discussions to Johannesburg and opened up an exchange between city leaders, experts, practitioners, and citizens. Because leaders from around the world are constantly looking for good practices to learn from, the festival contributed to a benchmarking process regarding ecomobility, sustainable development, and climate change mitigation and adaptation.

The EcoMobility Dialogues provided a platform for academics, decision-makers, and practitioners to exchange knowledge and experiences from case studies, common problems, and possible solutions in the form of policies, projects, and planning attempts. It became evident from all contributions that promoting walking, cycling, and public transport is essential for cities all over the world to combat climate change.

Because the Dialogues were hosted in the festival area, international mayors and other high-level city officials could test innovative ecomobile vehicles in the streets of Sandton. In a transport tour organised by the City of Johannesburg, Dialogue participants were sent from Sandton CBD to Soweto by minibus taxis, Gautrain, and bus rapid transit. The field trip enabled them to experience local circumstances and interact with actors working in the field of ecomobility, such as the bike empowerment centre in Soweto.

"We can learn from cities from all over the world. A lot of the learning in Johannesburg has been from Latin America and East Asia. In many African cities, you don't have the resources you have in the Global North. Within a much more constrained resource envelope, you can see creativity in everyday life of people finding ways to get around in the city. In the end, it is a combination of learning from the context with more resources and from the contexts with fewer resources than us, as well as those that are similar to us—for example, countries like Brazil."
Prof. Philip Harrison, University of the Witwatersrand, Johannesburg

"Some people come from places where such things happen very often. We want to tell them 'we have joined you and thank you for leading the way.' We have taken their experiences and made them unique, we have localised them, we have made them suitable for South Africa, which is very important. For those countries that are still to go on this journey, we have shown them that it can happen: it is possible to get your residents to change the way they move!"
Lisa Seftel, executive director of transport, City of Johannesburg

◁
Participants of the Mayors' Roundtable shortly before adopting the Declaration on Ecomobility in Cities

The Johannesburg Declaration on Ecomobility in Cities

Debates in a meeting of technical experts and a leadership roundtable led to the endorsement of the Declaration on Ecomobility in Cities. With the declaration, local governments take responsibility and recognise ecomobility as an integrated, socially inclusive, and environmentally friendly transport option that brings multiple benefits for people, cities, and the planet. The United Nations Environment Program (UNEP), The Partnership on Sustainable Low Carbon Transport (SloCaT), Walk21, and the Global Fund for Cities Development (FMDV) were amongst the declaration's first endorsers.

Parks Tau, the executive mayor of Johannesburg, presented the declaration at the COP21 in Paris, the twenty-first United Nations Climate Change Conference in December 2015. It will also be featured in the 2016 United Nations Conference on Housing and Sustainable Urban Development (HABITAT III) and other international conferences on sustainable cities, climate change mitigation, and people-friendly transport options.

"The Johannesburg Declaration on Ecomobility in Cities, adopted during the EcoMobility Festival, will serve as lead statement in future international discussions on mobility, climate change, and sustainable urban development."

Monika Zimmermann, deputy secretary general, ICLEI – Local Governments for Sustainability

"We cities are not going to Paris to say that climate change is a complex issue to solve. We'll bring solutions."

Parks Tau, executive mayor, City of Johannesburg

"In South Africa, transport is a major source of greenhouse gas emissions. In the Johannesburg Growth and Development Strategy, we focus on ecomobile modes. This strategy wants to commit to ecomobility as a mode of choice, as a way in which we can grow upon our lifestyle and mindset change, our behavioural change."

Alex Bhiman, transport department, City of Johannesburg

"The Johannesburg Declaration will play an important role for cities, influencing the common position and helping local leaders to take bold actions."

Kabir Mahmood, executive magistrate, Dhaka South Corporation, Bangladesh

▷ Along with Johannesburg, cities from South Korea, Brazil, Colombia, Mexico, Iceland, the Philippines, Malaysia, and Honduras were amongst the first to sign the declaration and take home the festival messages.

Edited version as of 29 October 2015

The Johannesburg Declaration on Ecomobility in Cities

October 2015, Johannesburg, South Africa

a world class African city

ICLEI
Local Governments for Sustainability

EcoMobility WorldFestival 2015

7 Festival results, reflections, and legacies

"What made the festival a success was the combination of three components: first, the bold communication campaign under the motto 'Change the way you move'; second, the month-long urban reality lab with a large-scale test-run for alternative traffic flows; third, the ongoing process of interactive and responsive planning and implementation, operating in real time. A key lesson learnt is that 'It can be done'—especially with leadership, strategic vision, and hands-on management in a cross-sectoral team."

Konrad Otto-Zimmermann,
creative director of the EcoMobility Festivals

▷
The temporary lanes dedicated to public transport will be made permanent in 2016.

▷
The shuttle services on the public transport loop were well received.
A permanent, dedicated lane will be implemented in the near future.

▷
The improvement of pedestrian and cycling infrastructure in Sandton will continue.

▷▷
The Rea Vaya will be extended from Johannesburg CBD to Alexandra and Sandton in 2017.

Measuring the change: the festival results

The EcoMobility World Festival 2015 mobilised the public of Johannesburg and beyond. The huge effort that businesses, commuters, and residents had to make raised public expectations with regard to the festival's actual impact. However, behavioural patterns rarely change overnight. In particular, diehard mobility habits are persistent. Thus, the results in numbers provide only a vague idea of the festival's long-term impact.

In order to measure the festival's short-term impact and whether its goals have been met, the City of Johannesburg closely monitored and evaluated each activity during the month. The primary objective of this evaluation was to assess the efficacy of the implemented transport measures and to learn from the experiences for future transport projects. The second objective was to measure the degree of awareness that the festival has created about ecomobility and other sustainability topics.

The city administration—together with consulting firms Arup and MPA and the Gauteng City-Region Observatory (GCRO)—conducted several surveys, measured travel times and speeds, and monitored the usage of cars and public transport. Furthermore, an analysis of the media uptake of the festival, including social media, was conducted by IBM Research South Africa.

The changed way of movement

The evaluation of the Transport Management Plan revealed that the festival saw significant changes in the way commuters moved to and inside Sandton CBD. While some ecomobile commuting modes were picked up quickly, the use of others remained lower than expected. A survey conducted during the festival revealed that only 15 per cent of the respondents changed their mode of travel and 9 per cent of respondents changed it for more than ten days of the month.

Festival Footprint

The festival successfully reduced the percentage of private-car usage in Sandton by 22 per cent, according to the Gauteng City-Region Observatory (GCRO). Access to all buildings was successfully maintained, and the managed access points well administered. To enable safe and easy walking and cycling, through traffic was limited in the centre of the CBD. However, the streets surrounding the loop became more congested.

Walking

Compared to a survey carried out in 2013, five times more people walked along West Street, the central axis through the CBD, which was turned into an ecomobile boulevard during the festival. A peak of 2,400 pedestrians per hour was recorded on West Street in one direction during the festival.

Last-mile services

While the tuk-tuks served passengers well as a last-mile service, the ecomobile last-mile services offered during the festival were poorly used. Also, fewer operators had offered their services than initially envisioned: only five out of more than ten operators who initially expressed interest provided services inside and outside the loop. Reasons were a lack of financial and other support for operations and technical setbacks of products offered, in terms of security, payment, tracking, and registration of the vehicles.

Transport loop

The festival's hop-on/hop-off minibus service on the public transport loop in the CBD was very well received by passengers. The dedicated lane for the loop was an effective testing ground for the future permanent Sandton transport loop.

If you changed your mode during the festival, what mode did you change to?

Source: Survey Monkey SCMB in partnership with Growthpoint and Arup, Oct 2015

30% Gautrain

19% Bus

 **10%** Walk

 9% Park & Ride

 8% Car pool

 8% Minibus

6% Cycle

 4% Metred Taxi

 3% Private Car

 3% Motorbike

Gautrain

The Gautrain increased its ridership by 13.9 per cent in October 2015, compared to September 2015. This increase translates to 1,031 passenger trips per day to and from Sandton Station. Assuming single-person car occupancy, 515 less cars entered Sandton per day.

Park & Ride and managed lanes

The Park & Ride sites resulted in a daily average of 700 fewer cars entering and leaving Sandton. People using Park & Ride facilities reported savings of ten to twenty minutes per trip in their regular commute. A survey conducted among Park & Ride users indicates that 47 per cent thought the festival was a success and a further 26 per cent thought that "accommodating people, not cars, created a more enjoyable environment". Moreover, 89 per cent of all respondents indicated that the managed lanes were an excellent idea and 69 per cent of them indicated that the managed lanes saved them time overall. Although those who used the facilities found it very useful, the take-up was poorer than expected—the City provided 10,000 spaces, but less than 1,000 were used on a daily basis. Some Park & Ride spots were highly frequented—including locations west of Sandton—while others were very poorly used.

Additional transportation services

The usage of the additional transportation services was much higher than the Park & Ride use itself because many people preferred to be dropped at the location or even walked there from home. Additional services from the west into Sandton were well used, such as the festival express buses; here operators are now considering permanently installing these express services. Other services were poorly used, so during the festival the City decided to make improvements by establishing more direct services to Sandton and to extend the free minibus taxi services. However, usage remained low for the rest of the festival month.

Cycle lanes

Unlike the recreational cycling events, commuter cycling to Sandton did not get much traction. No more than fifty people used cycle routes on weekdays. Many people were expecting dedicated cycling lanes rather than the demarcated routes provided. Consequently, people expressed that there was a lack of safety on these routes. The lack of shower and secure lockup facilities for cyclists was another deterrent. However, businesses are planning to provide such facilities for their employees in the future.

Carpooling

A survey indicates that 8 per cent of respondents decided to carpool during the festival. This could be one of the long-lasting changes in commuting to Sandton CBD, enhanced and promoted through car-sharing platforms. As Uber's popularity is increasing rapidly in Johannesburg, its ride-sharing option could play an important role in the future.

"I must applaud the City for having been bold and bringing us ecomobility. It was the first time that I saw and heard people inquire about public transport and routes. This was not only in Johannesburg—the idea of ecomobility spread all over the country. There were people as far as Cape Town and Durban that adopted ecomobility."
Ajen Sita, chief executive officer, Ernst & Young (EY)

"Interventions like the EcoMobility World Festival are an interesting test pilot for us to see what works and what doesn't work, and how we hardwire the things that do work into policy, so that the city continues to be sustainable."
Yondela Silimela, executive director, department of development planning, City of Johannesburg

"The EcoMobility Festival was never about achieving miraculous achievements overnight, but pointing out compelling global reasons and ways for citizens to contribute to decongestion in our urban cores."
Parks Tau, executive mayor, City of Johannesburg

Social media sentiments

The festival was widely discussed on social media platforms. Especially Twitter served as an indicator of people's opinions about the experiment. While most tweets were neutral about the festival, the positive statements prevailed over the negative sentiments. The transport modes offered were largely commented in a positive way, especially the Park & Ride facilities, Metrobus operations, and the possibilities of walking. Those who mentioned West Street in their tweets were entirely positive about ecomobility. The dedicated public transport lanes received a very high positive reception on Twitter, followed by the festival's security measures.

Under the hashtag #bridgecollapse, Twitter users first commented negatively on the collapse of scaffolding for the bridge that will connect Alexandra and Sandton from 2016. Four hours after the incident, Twitter sentiment had turned positive, highlighting the city administration's quick and comprehensive emergency management.

Reflections on the festival and lessons learnt

Besides actual numbers in commuter choices and transport modes used, the festival enabled many learning effects that will have a long lasting influence not only on the perception of public transport and infrastructure projects, but also on public debates in the city and the relationship between citizens, companies, and the city administration.

While there were many calls for safety, there was a growing appreciation that different road users are responsible for each other's safety, which can be built through greater awareness—for example, with cycle lanes or pedestrian infrastructure. During the festival month, improved walking facilities significantly increased pedestrian activity.

An important public debate and conversation on congestion, vehicle use and alternatives, environmental issues, and the role of transport accompanied the festival. There is a new consensus on the role of vehicles in congestion and climate change—and an increasing realisation that ordinary residents can make a difference.

The City and commuters realised that the full potential of public transport systems can be only revealed once the entire network is fully effective. The festival strengthened partnerships with transport operators, including the minibus taxi industry, as well as with business in Sandton. Some businesses took the campaign internally, encouraged their employees to adopt ecomobility, and offered services such as company shuttle buses. Residents' feedback was positive, leading to changed perceptions of using minibus taxis, Park & Ride sites, and the re-allocation of road space for managed lanes.

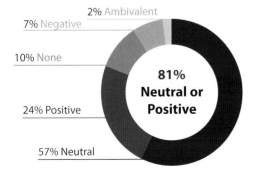

SOCIAL MEDIA STATISTICS

6,100 Participants
17,000 Tweets
5,800,000 Minimum reach
26,000,000 Average reach
350,000,000 Impressions

2% Ambivalent
7% Negative
10% None
24% Positive
57% Neutral

81% Neutral or Positive

_"_

Feeling less stressed after taking the gautrain bus today for #EcoMobility. #EcoMobilityMonth

_"_

- Twitter User

_"_

Actually funny how this EcoMobility thing has cleared congestion on the outskirts of Sandton CBD, William Nicol is such a breeze.

_"_

- Facebook User

Building change: ecomobility legacy projects in Johannesburg

The EcoMobility World Festival 2015 will leave a lasting legacy for Johannesburg and beyond. Building on the spirit of excitement that the festival brought to the region, the City of Johannesburg has decided to implement ten legacy projects that build on the experiences shared during the month of October 2015. Part of this legacy is the dedicated walking and cycling lane between Sandton and Alexandra—including the new bridge over the M1 motorway, and thirty kilometres of new sidewalks in Alexandra. Combined, the measures aim to provide a comprehensive multimodal transport system, which is a prerequisite for the aspired shift in attitudes and behaviours.
The legacy projects include:

Permanent public transport loop: In order to give way to public transport and to enhance comfort and safety for passengers, the temporary dedicated public transport lanes around and through the core of the Sandton CBD will become permanent and strictly enforced. The completed loop will include wider pedestrian walkways, road upgrades, soft and hard landscaping, improved road signage and street lighting, and commuter shelters.

Dedicated lanes for high-occupancy vehicles: Due to the success of the festival's managed lanes, permanent contraflow lanes for the smooth flow of buses, minibus taxis, and carpools will be implemented on the road link between Randburg and Sandton.

Express buses and permanent P&R facilities: Gautrain and Metrobus will continue their express bus services during peak hours to and from Sandton. Four Park & Ride facilities will be made permanent, with three of them serviced by Gautrain feeder buses.

Enhancement of walking and cycling infrastructure: Infrastructure for pedestrians and cyclists will be improved in Sandton. The pedestrian walkways and cycle lanes along Maude Street, between West Street and Rivonia Road, will be widened.

Marked cycle lane between business hubs: a cycle lane and a new bridge will be implemented between the Rosebank and Sandton in co-operation with Sandton's business community.

Bike distribution programme: The City's bike distribution programme will be enhanced towards the northernmost suburbs of Johannesburg, including Sandton and Alexandra. Schools and local organisations are partners for bike training events, donations, and bike empowerment centres.

Smartphone application: The festival app Vaya Moja will be further developed to provide information about public transport services and traffic conditions.

Dedication of street space to alternative uses: temporary road transformations for alternative uses will become regular in Johannesburg, including an annual Road Safety Family Day.

Extension of BRT into Sandton: The Rea Vaya services between Sandton, Alexandra, and the Johannesburg CBD and the introduction of feeder routes to extend the network to Rosebank, Randburg, Ivory Park, and Midrand are on the way. The new infrastructure will include dedicated BRT lanes, upgraded mixed traffic lanes, new pedestrian walkways, and improved street lighting and signage.

◁
Proposed pedestrian and
cycling bridge across
Sandton Drive

About

City of Johannesburg—www.joburg.org.za

With a population of 4.5 million, Johannesburg is the largest city in South Africa and the economic hub of southern Africa. The city leadership has embarked on ambitious programmes to overcome the social and spatial divide of the apartheid era, to strengthen the economy and alleviate poverty, and to create a green city for the sake of both enhancing quality of life and contributing to the global efforts towards a green planet.

ICLEI – Local Governments for Sustainability —www.iclei.org

ICLEI – Local Governments for Sustainability is the world's leading association of cities and local governments dedicated to sustainable development. It is a powerful movement of twelve megacities, one hundred supercities and urban regions, 450 large cities, and 450 medium-sized cities and towns in eighty-six countries. ICLEI's EcoMobility Program aims to promote the use of more public and non-motorised transportation, enhance the efficiency of vehicles, and use urban planning to improve transportation systems.

The Urban Idea—www.theurbanidea.com

The Urban Idea is a creative studio aiming to improve cities through creative concepts and innovative projects. The Urban Idea promotes EcoMobility as a new paradigm of urban mobility and urban transport planning. The studio applies the CityScene methodology to the promotion of ecomobility, by showcasing future sustainable urban mobility in a real city, with real people, in real time. The creative director leads the series of EcoMobility World Festivals.

Acknowledgements

Across the board: ICLEI – Local Governments for Sustainability, The Urban Idea, Sandton Management District, SADMON Projects & Consulting

Events: Freedom Ride, Discovery, Hollard, South African Police Services (SAPS), South African Breweries (SAB), road safety organisations

Exhibition: South African National Energy Development Institute (SANEDI), The Urban Idea, The Coloured Cube, Pure Grit, over thirty exhibitors

Dialogues: Hollard, Global Environment Facility (GEF), Industrial Development Corporation (IDC)

Transport: Public Utility Transport Corporation (PUTCO), Metrobus, South African National Taxi Council (SANTACO) Greater Johannesburg Region, Gautrain, MPA Consulting Engineers, Top Six Management, Arup, Bophelong, Lenash

Monitoring: Gauteng City-Region Observatory (GCRO), IBM, Arup, Newsclip, Growthpoint

City departments: Johannesburg Roads Agency, Johannesburg Metropolitan Police Department, Johannesburg Development Agency, City Parks, Group Communications, Transport, Joburg Property Company, Region E, Emergency Management Services, Community Development

Government: SANEDI, NDOT, Gauteng Department of Roads and Transport, Sandton SAPS

Volunteers: Harambee, 250 volunteers

Imprint

© 2016 by jovis Verlag GmbH
Texts by kind permission of the authors.
Pictures by kind permission of the photographers/holders of the picture rights.
All rights reserved.

Cover: Tobias Kuttler
Authors: Tobias Kuttler, Theresa Zimmermann
Editor: Konrad Otto-Zimmermann
Contributor: Andrew Kerr
Copy-editing: Inez Templeton
Proofreading: Mara Taylor
Lithography: Bild1Druck, Berlin
Design and Setting: jovis: Samuel Zwerger
Printing and binding: Graspo CZ, a.s., Zlín
Bibliographic information published by the Deutsche Nationalbibliothek
The Deutsche Nationalbibliothek lists this publication in the Deutsche Natio-nalbibliographie; detailed bibliographic data are available on the Internet at http://dnb.b-nb.de

jovis Verlag GmbH
Kurfürstenstraße 15/16
10785 Berlin

www.jovis.de

jovis books are available worldwide in selected bookstores. Please contact your nearest bookseller or visit www.jovis.de for information concerning your local distribution.

ISBN 978-3-86859-424-9

Festival Planners

Organiser
City of Johannesburg
Partner
ICLEI – Local Governments for Sustainability, with support from The Urban Idea GmbH
Creative director EcoMobility Festivals
Konrad Otto-Zimmermann

Picture Credits

COVER: Tobias Kuttler ▲, Simphiwe Nkwali ◣, ▼, ◢
aquatic creature/Shutterstock.com: 24
Barbara Breitsprecher: 4
B Brown/shutterstock.com: 42
Charrlotte Adelina: Author photo Tobias Kuttler
Daniel Huhn: 17▲, 37▼, 39▲, 43▼, 63, 68, 70, 71▲, ◣
Henrique NDR Martins / istockphoto.com: 61◢
ICLEI – Local Governments for Sustainability: 79
Itumeleng English: 2, 12, 18▶, 59◣
Johannesburg Development Agency, City of Johannesburg: 50◢, 80
Julian Isfort: 56▲
Kriang kan / Shutterstock.com: 60◣
Lungelo Mbulwana: 19▶, 55◣, 62◢
Madelene Cronje: 17◢, 62◀
Mounaim Rhozyel: Author photo Theresa Zimmermann
Simphiwe Nkwali: 6, 9, 10▲, ▼, 13◀, ▶, 16, 17◣, 18◀, 19◀, 20▼, ▲, ▶, 21, 23▼, ◣, 25, 31◢; 33◀, ◣, 36▼, 39◢; 41◢, 48, 51, 58, 59▶, 62◣, 64, 65▶, ◣, 67▼, 69, 71◢, 73▼, 74, 75, 76, 77, 78, 71◢, ◣
studioMAS Architects + Urban Designers: 85
The Coloured Cube: 53▼
The Urban Idea: 65▼, ◢
Tobias Kuttler: 11▲, ▶, ▼, 20◢, 23 ▶,◢, 26, 29▼, 30, 31▼, 32, 35, 36◢, 37▼, 38, 40, 41▼, ▶, 45, 47, 50▼, 52, 53▼, ▶, 54, 55▼, 56▼, 57, 60▶, 61▼,◣, 67◢, 81▼
Theresa Zimmermann: 20◀,◣, 22, 28, 29◣, 33◢, 41◣, 42▼, 43▲, 45◀, 59▼, 59◢, 72▼, 73▼, 81◢
GRAPHICS
Susan Yin: 5, 7, 8, 27▶, 46, 82, 84,
Tobias Kuttler: 14-15
MAPS
Tobias Kuttler: 12, 27◀, 32, 34, 49